THE RAW FOOD COOKBOOK

Jennie Reekie

THE KINGSWOOD PRESS

The Kingswood Press
an imprint of William Heinemann Ltd.
10 Upper Grosvenor Street, London W1X 9PA

LONDON   MELBOURNE
JOHANNESBURG   AUCKLAND

First published 1986

0 434 98086 2

Typeset by Deltatype, Ellesmere Port, South Wirral
Printed in Great Britain by
Redwood Burn Ltd., Trowbridge, Wiltshire

CONTENTS

INTRODUCTION

Why eat food raw? Surely when men and women have spent centuries perfecting the art of cooking, is this not a retrograde step? Is it not rather akin to returning to riding in horse-drawn vehicles and forgetting that the motor car had ever been invented?

The answer is, quite simply, that not only is raw food delicious, but it is undeniably better for you than any form of cooked food. There are also a few other useful spin-offs: it is generally very quick and simple to prepare, and may also help reduce your fuel bills!

I am certainly not suggesting that you should never eat any cooked food again. If, however, you increase your intake of raw food as against cooked, not only should you feel healthier, but you may well find that without making any apparent effort, you have lost some weight as well. One of the reasons for this is that raw food is more filling and satisfying than cooked. A 100 g/4 oz cooked steak or fillet of fish looks fairly puny, but after eating that quantity of raw meat or fish, you will feel very replete. Vegetables are also much more filling when they are raw – one has only to think of what 450 g/1 lb spinach looks like when raw, and then the pathetically small amount that is left in the pan when it is cooked. Not only are you throwing away half the goodness with the cooking liquor, but you have to buy so much more in the first place.

A balanced diet is all important. Unless you happen to be in a high health-risk category (for example, overweight and/or high blood pressure), it should not be necessary to completely cut out butter, cream and other dairy fats to maintain a reasonably low blood cholestrol level – if you eat more raw food. Raw food will increase your intake of fibre, and will also reduce your cholestrol intake from cooked foods, such as meat fat, gravies, sauces, eggs, buttered vegetables and pastries.

There is also increasing concern throughout the Western world about the number of chemical additives put into our food. It is an extremely complex problem in which both sides seem able to produce valid arguments. Most of us feel, though, that we would rather eat the minimum amount possible of these substances, and while eating raw food does not completely resolve the issue, if you use good, fresh ingredients, the amount of additives you are exposed to will be considerably reduced.

A great misconception still exists, however, that raw food is either very dull and boring (the 'eating like a rabbit' syndrome), or, at the other extreme, that it is far too esoteric for every day. It is true that lettuce, caviare and oysters are all raw food, but the latter two scarcely feature in my diet. While I enjoy lettuce, I never eat it just on its own, but combine it with other vegetables, herbs and good-flavoured dressing. I am sure these pages will prove that raw food is not only healthy, but interesting and delicious as well.

Jennie Reekie

DRESSINGS AND DIPS

In the creation of a salad, the dressing is generally more important than the ingredients it dresses. A dressing can either transform what might be considered mundane vegetables and fruit into a memorable dish, or it can completely mar some superb basic ingredients.

This does not mean that all dressings have to be made with the most expensive ingredients. Although dressings made with the finest Vièrge olive and walnut oils are a food experience, one would not want to eat them every day. You can make equally good dressings with sunflower or safflower oil and, depending on the recipe, these may actually complement the other ingredients better.

All food is volatile, and it is always difficult to be specific about quantities, but this is particularly true when it comes to making dressings. One brand of oil may be slightly different to another depending on its country of origin, and vinegars vary enormously in their acidity. If you are using a citrus juice, the difference is even greater: just as oranges vary considerably in their sweetness, so do lemons and limes. It is therefore important to always taste and adjust accordingly, adding perhaps a few more drops of vinegar or lemon juice, or a teaspoon more oil.

In the 1960s, dips were something that were always made with cheese, accompanied by crisps (which generally broke when one dipped them into the mixture), and served at cocktail parties. Since then the dip has gone through a complete metamorphosis and has emerged as a dish accompanied by raw vegetables (crudités), which can be served not just as a nibble at a party or before a meal, but as a starter, a light meal, or part of a buffet or simple family meal.

Many of the recipes for dips are actually classic recipes from other cultures and cuisines which were served as sauces or hors d'oeuvres, such as aioli, taramasalata and tapénade, which we have adapted. Whilst the most usual crudités are sticks of cucumber, carrot and celery, radishes, cauliflower florets and strips of red and green pepper, this is only the tip of the iceberg of what can be used: try little florets of purple sprouting broccoli or calabrese; mange tout (snow peas); sticks of young turnip, kohlrabi, mooli and celeriac (although the latter must first be quickly dipped in some lemon juice to preserve the colour); courgettes (zucchini); French beans and runner beans; spinach stalks and crisp chicory leaves.

Oils

Oils are most usually consumed on raw food as a dressing for a salad, and there are a number of different oils on the market. Most of them are recommended as being suitable for salads, but some are better than others, so the most common ones are listed here, together with some comments on how they are best used, and how much polyunsaturate they contain. In addition to the specific oils such as sunflower and soya bean, there are some oils just labelled 'vegetable'. These should be avoided as they are likely to contain a high percentage of coconut oil which is highly saturated.

It is now universally accepted that saturated fats and oils increase the cholestrol level in the blood, causing hardening of the arteries and, consequently, heart disease. Polyunsaturated oils on the other hand will, if anything, help reduce the cholestrol level in the blood and, provided you do not eat too much of them, are good for you. In between the good and the bad there are a few monounsaturated oils – olive oil is the best known – which are neither harmful nor particularly healthy.

Grape Seed Oil This is a fairly new polyunsaturated oil on the

2

market. It is a high quality oil which is almost flavourless, and so is suitable for a French dressing to which you are going to add strong-flavoured ingredients such as herbs, mustard, etc. As it is quite expensive, I feel it would be slightly wasted in a mayonnaise.

Olive Oil This is undoubtedly the most popular salad oil and comes in several different grades, of which the finest is Vièrge or even 'extra Vièrge', which is extracted from the olives by cold pressing. It is usually a bright green colour and, as it is very expensive, should be reserved for dishes in which you need a small quantity of oil, but really want all the pungency it can provide. The other grades vary considerably and it is worth buying small bottles of several different brands to find out which you prefer before buying a large bottle or can, which are more economical. If you want a slight olive oil flavour, but do not want it to be too strong, you can use a mixture of olive and sunflower or grape seed oil. The first combination is particularly good in mayonnaise.

Rape-Seed Oil Those brilliant fields of yellow which have become such a feature of the countryside in the late spring produce seeds in the autumn from which oil is extracted. High in the league of polyunsaturates, it is the constituent of many polyunsaturate margarines, but I find it has a slightly unpleasant after-taste and is not really suitable for dressings.

Safflower Oil This has the highest percentage of polyunsaturates – 78%. A very pure oil, it is excellent for all forms of French dressing, but again it is expensive, so would not really be suitable for mayonnaise.

Sesame Seed Oil This oil has been used for centuries in the East, and those immortal words in Aladdin, 'Open Sesame', refer to the vast vats in which it was stored. There are two types of sesame oil, the dark brown variety, which is made from the roasted seeds, and is used extensively in Chinese cookery, and the clearer, yellow kind, which is prepared from the unroasted seeds. The former has a very strong flavour and a small quantity added to another oil, as in the Oriental dressing (page 8) will give a strong sesame flavour. The oil made from unroasted seeds, which is usually available in health food stores, does not have such a defined flavour and so can be used to make a dressing without being combined with other oils, or again it can be mixed with another oil for a dressing with just a hint of sesame. It is not as high in polyunsaturates as some of the other oils, containing more monounsaturates.

Soya Bean Oil   This has been used for over 4,000 years in China, and although not as high in polyunsaturates as sunflower and safflower, it is still very much in the 'first division'. It has a slight after-taste for plain French dressings, but makes excellent mayonnaise.

Sunflower Oil   This is one of the most useful oils for everyday salad dressings and mayonnaise. High in polyunsaturates, it has very little flavour and therefore combines well with some of the stronger oils to give a delicate dressing.

Walnut and Hazelnut Oil

I think they have the most superb flavour of any oils, but their big drawback is that they are very expensive, and so may only be suitable as a 'treat'. Again there are different grades and there are some which are also mixed with a vegetable oil. However, I feel rather than do this, I would prefer to buy a pure nut oil and mix it with another oil of my choice to make it more economical. Once opened, these oils go 'off' very quickly if they are left at room temperature, and so should be stored in the refrigerator. Walnut oil is high in polyunsaturates; hazlenut has more monounsaturates.

To make Yogurt

The recipe for making yogurt is included here, as it forms the basis of many dressings, as well as being used in both sweet and savoury recipes. Although there are a number of yogurt-making machines on the market which keep the yogurt at a controlled temperature whilst it is setting, this is not essential provided you have a suitable warm place to leave the yogurt to set. The back of an Aga or other solid fuel cooker is ideal, but you can just as well use the airing cupboard, or even beside the pilot light on a gas cooker.

All yogurt is alive and contains a bacillus, so you must have some natural yogurt in order to start making your own. Bring 500 ml/1 pint of either whole or skimmed milk slowly up to boiling point, then remove from the heat. When it has cooled to blood temperature, stir in three tablespoons of natural yogurt and blend it really well. Do not add the yogurt when the milk is still very hot as this will kill the bacillus.

Pour the milk into individual pots, cover and put into a warm place. Leave for eight to twelve hours, or until the yogurt has set, then put into the refrigerator to chill. It will keep well for several days. Once you have started the chain, always remember to keep back three tablespoons of yogurt for making the next batch.

French Dressing

Undoubtedly the most useful basic dressing. On page two the various suitable oils are discussed.

The acid content, however, whether it is red or white wine vinegar, tarragon vinegar, raspberry or other fruit vinegar, cider vinegar, or citrus juice such as lime, lemon or even orange juice, is just as important to the final flavour. What is chosen will depend on a number of factors – personal preference being the paramount one –but also what is to be dressed: if a little is to be sprinkled over some slices of dried meat, you will probably want red wine vinegar; if making a salad to serve with fish, tarragon vinegar would be a good choice; while if wanting a sharp dressing for a salad with a high proportion of fruit in it, cider vinegar would be excellent.

Here is a very basic recipe to which can be added chopped fresh herbs, crushed garlic, spices such as crushed coriander, or any other little quirk that appeals to you at the time. Always remember that in most cases the dressing is meant to compliment the salad, not dominate it.

METRIC/IMPERIAL
3 *tablespoons oil (page 2)*
1–1½ *tablespoons vinegar or*
   citrus juice (see above)
¼ *teaspoon French mustard*
salt and freshly milled black
   pepper
a pinch of sugar (optional)

AMERICAN
3 *tablespoons oil (page 2)*
1–1½ *tablespoons vinegar or*
   citrus juice (see above)
¼ *teaspoon French mustard*
salt and freshly milled black
   pepper
a pinch of sugar (optional)

Although you can whisk all the ingredients together in a basin, the easiest way is simply to put them all into a screw-topped jar, screw it up tightly and then shake well. I often use an old Meaux mustard pot which makes a quite attractive container, using the last of the mustard to make the dressing.

Mayonnaise

Before the advent of blenders and food processors which can emulsify whole eggs and oil at an incredibly high speed, mayonnaise could only be made with egg yolks. This creates a much richer sauce than that made using a whole egg, and using egg yolks only increases the proportion of cholesterol.

For some recipes, traditional mayonnaise is just too rich and heavy and a blender mayonnaise is preferable, especially if the mayonnaise is helping to add 'bulk' to something like a mousse. However, if you are making a simple dip for crudités, or require just a couple of tablespoons to give flavour to another sauce or dressing, then a traditional mayonnaise is better. On the whole, which one you use is very much a matter of personal preference, but in recipes where I feel it is important to use either one or the other, I have stated it.

Traditional Method:

METRIC/IMPERIAL	AMERICAN
2 egg yolks	2 egg yolks
salt and freshly milled black pepper	salt and freshly milled black pepper
½ teaspoon French mustard	½ teaspoon French mustard
2 tablespoons wine vinegar	2 tablespoons wine vinegar
300 ml/½ pint oil (see page 2)	1¼ cups oil (see page 2)

Put the egg yolks, seasoning, mustard and one tablespoon of the vinegar into a basin. Using either a wooden spoon or a balloon whisk (whichever you find easier – I find with a whisk there is less chance of it curdling), mix until they are well blended. Beat in the oil gradually, drop by drop until you have added about half of it and the mixture is beginning to look thick and shiny, then beat in the remainder of the oil a little more quickly. When all the oil has been incorporated, beat in the remaining vinegar. Taste and adjust the seasoning.

Note: There is no reason why this mixture cannot also be made in a blender, or a food processor. However, if using a processor, I have found a greater tendency for it to curdle as the egg yolks do not whisk up in the same way as does a whole egg. They remain below the blade and so do not emulsify well with the oil, unless you make a larger quantity with three or four egg yolks.

Blender Mayonnaise

METRIC/IMPERIAL	AMERICAN
1 egg	1 egg
salt and freshly milled black pepper	salt and freshly milled black pepper
½ teaspoon French mustard	½ teaspoon French mustard
2 tablespoons wine vinegar	2 tablespoons wine vinegar
300 ml/½ pint oil (see page 2)	1½ cups oil (see page 2)

Break the egg into the blender or food processor, add the seasoning, mustard and all the vinegar. Put on the lid and switch to high speed. If using a blender, remove the plug in the lid, or if using a food processor, remove the plunger. Keeping the motor running at high speed, pour in the oil in a very slow, steady stream until it has all been incorporated and the sauce is thick and smooth. Taste and adjust the seasoning.

Pawpaw Seed Dressing

Pawpaws (or papayas as they are also known) are almost the staple diet of a number of tropical countries, for both people and animals. A friend of mine who spent a year living in Tonga told me that the dogs there (and apparently every family has at least one) were never fed on meat which was far too scarce and expensive, but lived entirely on pawpaws.

They are extremely beneficial to the digestive system. They contain an enzyme which closely resembles pepsin which is produced in the stomach naturally, and helps the digestion of proteins. By the same process the enzyme also has the effect of tenderizing meat, by breaking down its fibres. The flesh, skin and seeds can all be used for this purpose and pawpaw is the main constituent in a number of commercial meat tenderizers.

METRIC/IMPERIAL	AMERICAN
200 ml/8 fl oz sunflower oil	1 cup sunflower oil
100 ml/4 fl oz tarragon vinegar	½ cup tarragon vinegar
2 slightly rounded tablespoons raw sugar	2 slightly rounded tablespoons raw sugar
½ teaspoon salt	½ teaspoon salt
1 teaspoon dry mustard	1 teaspoon dry mustard
½ small onion	½ small onion
the seeds of 1 pawpaw (about 3 tablespoons)	the seeds of 1 pawpaw (about 3 tablespoons)

Put all the ingredients except the pawpaw seeds into a blender or food processor, and whizz until well emulsified. Add the pawpaw seeds and whizz again until they are coarsely crushed. This makes a large quantity of dressing, but it will keep in a container in the refrigerator for a couple of weeks.

Oriental Dressing

Although this dressing obviously combines well with 'oriental' ingredients, such as bean sprouts, mooli and Chinese leaves, it makes an interesting variation as a dressing for the more classic

European and American salad ingredients. If you like, you can replace one teaspoon of the oil with a teaspoon of brown sesame oil.

METRIC/IMPERIAL
3 tablespoons soya bean or
  sunflower oil
1½ tablespoons wine vinegar
2 teaspoons soy sauce
1 teaspoon very finely chopped
  ginger

AMERICAN
3 tablespoons soya bean or
  sunflower oil
1½ tablespoons wine vinegar
2 teaspoons soy sauce
1 teaspoon very finely chopped
  ginger

Put all the ingredients into a small basin and whisk thoroughly with a balloon whisk to emulsify them.

Cassis Dressing

This will appeal to anyone who likes a sweet and sour dressing, and it is excellent for a simple green salad to which some freshly chopped mint or basil has been added.

METRIC/IMPERIAL
3 tablespoons olive oil
1 tablespoon wine vinegar
1 tablespoon Crème de Cassis
salt and freshly milled black
  pepper

AMERICAN
3 tablespoons olive oil
1 tablespoon wine vinegar
1 tablespoon Crème de Cassis
salt and freshly milled black
  pepper

Put all the ingredients into a screw-topped jar and shake until they are well emulsified.

Ravigote Sauce

This watercress and herb sauce is excellent with salami or other cold meats, and also makes a good dressing for tomatoes.

METRIC/IMPERIAL	AMERICAN
½ bunch watercress	½ bunch watercress
1 clove garlic	1 clove garlic
1 tablespoon chopped parsley	1 tablespoon chopped parsley
1 tablespoon chopped chives	1 tablespoon chopped chives
1 tablespoon chopped tarragon	1 tablespoon chopped tarragon
1 tablespoon chopped chervil	1 tablespoon chopped chervil
1 teaspoon anchovy purée	1 teaspoon anchovy purée
2 tablespoons wine vinegar	2 tablespoon wine vinegar
½ teaspoon French mustard	½ teaspoon French mustard
150 ml/¼ pint olive oil	⅝ cup olive oil
freshly milled black pepper	freshly milled black pepper
salt (see method)	salt (see method)

Chop off 2.5 cm/1 inch of the watercress stalks and crush the garlic. Put all the ingredients, except the salt, into a blender or food processor and whizz until they form a smooth purée. Taste, and add a little salt if necessary.

Greek Lime Sauce

Now that fresh limes are readily available throughout the year, this makes a good alternative to a more classic French dressing for salads, and is also excellent sprinkled on air-dried meat (page 60–61). It keeps well in the refrigerator in a screw-topped jar.

METRIC/IMPERIAL	AMERICAN
150 ml/¼ pint fresh lime juice	⅝ cup fresh lime juice

150 ml/¼ pint olive oil	⅝ cup olive oil
150 ml/¼ pint clear honey	⅝ cup clear honey
1 teaspoon paprika	1 teaspoon paprika
salt	salt

Put all the ingredients except the salt into a blender or food processor and whizz together for about 30 seconds. Season to taste with salt.

Yogurt and Chive Dressing

This dressing combines especially well with root vegetables.

METRIC/IMPERIAL	AMERICAN
150 ml/¼ pint natural yogurt	⅝ cup natural yogurt
1 tablespoon olive oil	1 tablespoon olive oil
1 teaspoon Dijon mustard	1 teaspoon Dijon mustard
2 tablespoons chopped chives	2 tablespoons chopped chives
1 tablespoon chopped parsley	1 tablespoon chopped parsley
salt and freshly milled black pepper	salt and freshly milled black pepper.

Turn the yogurt into a basin, then stir in the oil and mustard, followed by the remaining ingredients, seasoning to taste with salt and pepper.

Rémoulade Sauce

Although rémoulade sauce is a classic accompaniment to grilled meat and fish, it is very good with air-dried meat (see page 60) as

11

well as being combined with chopped celery or thin slivers of celeriac, to make Celery or Celeriac Rémoulade.

METRIC/IMPERIAL	AMERICAN
300 ml/½ pint mayonnaise (page 6)	1¼ cups mayonnaise (page 6)
2 teaspoons French mustard	2 teaspoons French mustard
2 teaspoons finely chopped capers	2 teaspoons finely chopped capers
1 teaspoon chopped parsley	1 teaspoon chopped parsley
1 teaspoon chopped tarragon	1 teaspoon chopped tarragon
1 teaspoon chopped chervil	1 teaspoon chopped chervil

Turn the mayonnaise into a basin, blend in all the remaining ingredients and leave for 30 minutes for the flavours to infuse before serving.

Tomato and Basil Mayonnaise

I originally devised this sauce to go with the sesame seed meat balls on page 65, but thought it was so good, that it was worth including as a recipe in its own right as it would be excellent with any of the air-dried or smoked meats, or even with fish that had been macerated in lime or lemon juice.

For the mayonnaise base it is best to use a light, blender mayonnaise made with sunflower or soya bean oil.

METRIC/IMPERIAL	AMERICAN
150 ml/¼ pint blender mayonnaise (page 17)	⅝ cup blender mayonnaise (page 17)
2 medium-sized tomatoes	2 medium-sized tomatoes
2–3 sprigs basil	2–3 sprigs basil
1 small clove garlic	1 small clove garlic
salt and feshly milled black pepper	salt and freshly milled black pepper

Put the mayonnaise into a blender or food processor. Plunge the tomatoes in boiling water for 30 seconds to loosen the skins, and then peel. Cut them into quarters. Very roughly chop the basil, discarding the tough stalks, and crush the garlic. Add them to the mayonnaise and whizz quickly to chop the tomatoes and basil, but do not completely purée them as the texture of the sauce is better if some small pieces of tomato are left in it. Season to taste.

Walnut Sauce

This sauce can be used in place of a walnut oil-based French dressing, and is excellent with simple green salads or with shredded red and green cabbage.

METRIC/IMPERIAL	AMERICAN
25 g/1 oz walnuts	¼ cup walnuts
4 tablespoons olive oil	4 tablespoons olive oil
1½ tablespoons wine vinegar	1½ tablespoons wine vinegar
1 rounded teaspoon Meaux or a similar mild-flavoured grain mustard	1 rounded teaspoon Meaux or a similar mild-flavoured grain mustard
2 teaspoons Parmesan cheese	2 teaspoons Parmesan cheese
salt and freshly milled black pepper	salt and freshly milled black pepper.

Finely grind the walnuts in a blender or food processor. Put into a screw-topped jar with all the remaining ingredients and shake well.

Austrian Soured Cream Dressing

Soured cream is used extensively throughout Germany, Austria and the Balkans, and this light dressing is excellent in coleslaw in place of mayonnaise.

METRIC/IMPERIAL	AMERICAN
1 egg yolk	1 egg yolk
2 tablespoons wine vinegar	2 tablespoons wine vinegar
300 ml/½ pint soured cream	1¼ cups sour cream
1 tablespoon chopped chives	1 tablespoon chopped chives
salt and freshly milled black pepper	salt and freshly milled black pepper

Blend the egg yolk, then beat in the vinegar. Stir in the cream and chives or spring onions and blend well. Season to taste with salt and pepper.

Tahina and Yogurt

Tahina, which is a paste made from pounded sesame seeds, crops up all the time in Middle Eastern cookery. It can be found in any Greek delicatessen and in most health food stores.

This 'salad' as it is described, can be served in exactly the same way as hummus and taramasalata: as a starter with strips of hot warm pitta or Arab bread. But it can also be served as a dip with crudités, is excellent as a sauce for pickled fish and, if it is thinned down further with some water, makes a superb salad dressing, especially for cabbage and firm lettuce-based salads.

METRIC/IMPERIAL	AMERICAN
150 ml/¼ pint tahina	⅝ cup tahina
150 ml/¼ pint natural yogurt	⅝ cup natural yogurt
2 cloves garlic	2 cloves garlic
juice 1 large lemon	juice 1 large lemon
1 tablespoon olive oil, preferably a virgin oil	1 tablespoon olive oil, preferably a virgin oil
about 3 tablespoons water	about 3 tablespoons water
2 tablespoons chopped parsley	2 tablespoons chopped parsley
salt and freshly milled black pepper.	salt and freshly milled black pepper

Blend the tahina with the yogurt in a basin. Crush the garlic and stir in with the lemon juice. Slowly stir in the oil, then the water, bit by bit. (The exact amount of water will depend on how you wish to serve the end result: it will need to be thicker if serving it as a dip, than if serving with pitta.) Add the parsley, and season to taste with salt and pepper.

Serves 4–6

Cucumber with Yogurt

The combination of yogurt, cucumber and mint appears in cuisines all over the world. In Greece it is called Tzatziki, in Turkey Cacik and in India, Raita. It can be served as an hors d'oeuvre, a dressing, or as a chutney.

METRIC/IMPERIAL	AMERICAN
½ large cucumber	½ large cucumber
½ teaspoon salt	½ teaspoon salt
300 ml/½ pint natural yogurt	1¼ cups natural yogurt
2 cloves garlic	2 cloves garlic
2 tablespoons chopped mint	2 tablespoons chopped mint
freshly milled black pepper	freshly milled black pepper

Finely dice the cucumber, put into a colander, sprinkle with the salt and leave to drain for 30 minutes. Put into a bowl and stir in the yogurt. Crush the cloves of garlic and add to the cucumber and yogurt, together with the mint and plenty of freshly milled black pepper.

Serves 4

Aioli

Often described as the 'Butter of Provence', I can well remember the first time I ever tried it, when I was working as an au pair in the South of France. To celebrate a saint's day the entire village attended lunch, which was held in the central square. It was all beautifully set out with tables with white cloths on them and wooden benches and the *pièce de résistance* was the pungent aioli served with cold cod and a tossed green salad.

METRIC/IMPERIAL	AMERICAN
3–4 *cloves garlic*	3–4 *cloves garlic*
2 *egg yolks*	2 *egg yolks*
salt and freshly milled black pepper	*salt and freshly milled black pepper*
300 *ml/½ pint olive oil*	1¼ *cups olive oil*

Crush the garlic and put into a basin with the egg yolks and seasoning and beat well. Gradually add the oil, drop by drop, as if making mayonnaise (see page 6). When all the oil has been incorporated, taste and adjust the seasoning accordingly.

Mexican Dip

Although excellent with crudités, this dip is particularly good with a little 'cooked' food in the form of corn chips.

METRIC/IMPERIAL	AMERICAN
450 *g/1 lb tomatoes*	1 *lb tomatoes*
½ *green chilli*	½ *green chilli*
2 *cloves garlic*	2 *cloves garlic*
1 *rounded tablespoon chopped coriander*	1 *rounded tablespoon chopped coriander*
salt and freshly milled black pepper	*salt and freshly milled black pepper*

Skin the tomatoes, cut them into quarters and remove the pips. Chop the flesh finely, then turn into a basin and mash lightly – you do not want to end up with a purée, but it should be slightly pulped. Very finely chop the chilli, discarding the seeds, crush the garlic and add to the tomatoes with the coriander and chilli. Mix well, then season to taste with salt and pepper and turn into a small serving dish.

Tapénade

A Provencal speciality, the name being derived from the local dialect – *tapeno* being the word for caper. It is a purée of olives, anchovies and capers, about which you either tend to be passionate, or simply loathe, according to how much you like the three basic ingredients!

The proportions can be varied according to personal preference, with more olive oil added to make a lighter, slightly less rich version. Serve it as a dip with crudités, hot toast, strips of pitta or crusty French bread. Another good way to serve it is as a dip or sauce, blending it with mayonnaise using the proportion of two parts mayonnaise to one part tapénade.

It stores for up to three months in the refrigerator. Pack into a small jar, pour over a little olive oil to seal it, and then close the jar.

METRIC/IMPERIAL	AMERICAN
225 g/8 oz black olives	2 cups black olives
4 large anchovy fillets	4 large anchovy fillets
2 slightly rounded tablespoons capers	2 slightly rounded tablespoons capers
a squeeze of lemon juice	a squeeze of lemon juice
4 tablespoons olive oil	4 tablespoons olive oil
freshly milled black pepper	freshly milled black pepper

Stone the olives, preferably using an olive or cherry stoner, or failing that by peeling off the flesh with a knife. Put the olives, anchovy fillets, capers and lemon juice into a blender or food processor and blend until smooth. Keeping the motor running, gradually pour in the olive oil, in a thin, steady stream, as if making mayonnaise. Season to taste with black pepper.

Italian Dip

This can be served with any crudités you like, but I find carrot and celery sticks are extremely good.

METRIC/IMPERIAL	AMERICAN
2 *cloves garlic*	2 *cloves garlic*
100 *g/4 oz walnuts*	1 *cup walnuts*
65 *g/1 ½ oz grated Parmesan cheese*	¼ *cup grated Parmesan cheese*
juice of 1 lemon	*juice of 1 lemon*
2 *tablespoons olive oil*	2 *tablespoons olive oil*
2 *tablespoons water*	2 *tablespoons water*
freshly milled black pepper	*freshly milled black pepper*

Put the peeled garlic and walnuts into a food processor. Grind until smooth, then keeping the motor running, add the Parmesan cheese and lemon juice, followed by the oil a tablespoon at a time, and finally the water. Season to taste with freshly milled black pepper.

Speedy Dip

When Lymeswold cheese made its appearance in 1983 it was the first time a soft Continental-type cheese had been made in the U.K. It has been extremely successful, but should you have difficulty in obtaining it, a soft Blue Brie or similar cheese could be substituted.

DRESSINGS AND DIPS

METRIC/IMPERIAL
100 g/4 oz Lymeswold cheese
150 ml/¼ pint soured cream
freshly milled black pepper
To garnish:
a little paprika

AMERICAN
4 oz Lymeswold cheese
⅝ cup sour cream
freshly milled black pepper
To garnish:
a little paprika

Mash the cheese well, then beat in the cream. Season with plenty of freshly milled black pepper. Turn into a serving dish and garnish with the paprika before serving.

SOUPS, VEGETABLE COCKTAILS AND SAVOURY ICES

This chapter could almost be 'the tomato chapter', as so many of the recipes are tomato-based: tomatoes, being technically a fruit rather than a vegetable, produce a considerable amount of juice, and therefore make a perfect base for a vegetable soup. I have experimented with making soups based on carrot and celery, ground up in a food processor, but to be quite honest, while they must be extremely healthy, I did not like the flavour and texture. They epitomised for me the very worst of health food: this book is essentially about food that tastes good and is generally healthy, rather than food which is supremely healthy, but regrettably does not taste very pleasant.

If you want to make vegetable and fruit juices extensively (both of which are a good basis for soup), you really need to purchase a special juicer. These have either a hydraulic press, or work on a centrifugal basis, and are the only means of efficiently extracting juice from fruit and vegetables other than citrus fruit. However, for the ordinary 'raw cook', the only really essential piece of equipment, other than the usual sharp knives, chopping boards, whisk, etc. is a blender, or even better still, a food processor. There are so many raw food recipes which require food to be puréed, ground or pounded which takes only seconds or minutes in a food processor.

Doing the same job by hand not only takes more time, but in the end, possibly because you are in a hurry, or your arm begins to ache, you do not end up with such a satisfactory result. In some cases, by using a food processor, you also increase the nutritional content. For example, for tomato juices and soups, it was always traditional to first peel the tomatoes and then to sieve them. Much of the mineral and vitamin content of the fruit lies in and just under the skin, and this is lost if the tomatoes are peeled. I find, that by using a processor, peeling is not necessary as the majority of the skin beccomes very finely ground. If the end result is meant to have a rough texture, like a gazpacho (see page 23), any large pieces can quite happily be left in, but if you do want it to be completely smooth, you can then sieve the purée, allowing the fine pieces to pass through the sieve and leaving only the large bits behind.

As well as soups – and they are not all tomato-based – there are recipes using cucumbers, avocados and clams as well as fruit. This chapter also contains a vegetable 'pick-me-up', a couple of tomato ices and, because it did not seem to fit in anywhere else, one of my favourite recipes – tomato jelly. If one is being a complete 'purist', gelatine should not be used in a raw book, but I feel its inclusion is justified by the fact that it enables one to make a greater number of interesting raw dishes, both sweet and savoury. If you wish to increase the amount of raw food you eat yourself and serve to your family and friends, it is essential that the food not only tastes good, but is as varied as possible, so that you do not get bored with it.

I always used powdered gelatine (gelatin) as I think it is the easiest form to use. If you are a vegetarian, you may prefer to use agar agar or carrageen moss, following the instructions on the packet. Where 15 g/½ oz or 1 envelope is given in the following recipes, use an equivalent amount to set 600 ml/1 pint of liquid.

Watercress and Tomato Soup

The watercress gives this tomato-based soup a slightly peppery taste.

METRIC/IMPERIAL	AMERICAN
1 large bunch watercress	1 large bunch watercress
450 g/1 lb tomatoes	1 lb tomatoes
1 small head of fennel	1 small head of fennel
1 tablespoon wine vinegar	1 tablespoon wine vinegar
150 ml/¼ pint water	⅝ cup water
salt and freshly milled black pepper	salt and freshly milled black pepper

Very roughly chop the watercress, tomatoes and fennel, and put into a blender or food processor and whizz until smooth. Add the vinegar and water and whizz again, then season to taste with salt and pepper. Turn into a serving bowl and chill until ready to serve.

Serves 4

Tomato and Orange Soup

A super-speedy soup if you are in a hurry.

METRIC/IMPERIAL	AMERICAN
600 ml/1 pint tomato juice	2½ cups tomato juice
150 ml/¼ pint orange juice	⅝ cup orange juice
1 generous tablespoon chopped dill	1 generous tablespoon chopped dill
1 tablespoon chopped chives	1 tablespoon chopped chives
salt and freshly milled black pepper	salt and freshly milled black pepper
To garnish:	To garnish:
4–6 tablespoons single cream	4–6 tablespoons light cream

Mix together the tomato and orange juice, add the dill and chives and season to taste with a little salt if necessary, and plenty of freshly milled black pepper. Divide between four to six bowls and chill until ready to serve. Just before serving, gently pour a tablespoon of cream into each bowl to make a decorative pattern.

Serves 4–6

Gazpacho

There are probably more different recipes for this soup than there are towns in Spain, although the basic ingredients of tomatoe, cucumber and pepper remain fairly constant.

METRIC/IMPERIAL	AMERICAN
450 g/1 lb ripe tomatoes	1 lb ripe tomatoes
1 green pepper	1 green pepper
1 onion	1 onion
½ cucumber	½ cucumber
2 cloves garlic	2 cloves garlic
4 tablespoons red wine vinegar	4 tablespoons red wine vinegar
3 tablespoons olive oil	3 tablespoons olive oil
3 tablespoons water	3 tablespoons water
salt and freshly milled black pepper	salt and freshly milled black pepper

Halve the tomatoes, halve the pepper and discard the core and seeds, peel the onion and halve, cut the cucumber into about eight pieces and crush the garlic. Put all the ingredients into a large blender or food processor. (If you only have a small blender, you may have to do this in two batches.) Purée until very smooth, then season to taste.

Chill for at least one hour until ready to serve, when you can serve it with the classic gazpacho accompaniments of croutons of bread, finely chopped onion, pepper and cucumber, but this is a good chunky version and I think it tastes good just on its own.

Serves 4–6

Cream of Tomato and Basil Soup

A low-calorie soup you can literally make in minutes in a blender or food processor.

METRIC/IMPERIAL	AMERICAN
450 g/1 lb ripe tomatoes	1 lb ripe tomatoes
225 g/8 oz low fat German style curd cheese	1 cup low fat German style curd cheese
2 large sprigs of basil	2 large sprigs of basil
1 teaspoon Worcestershire sauce	1 teaspoon Worcestershire sauce
salt and freshly milled black pepper	salt and freshly milled black pepper

Roughly chop the tomatoes and put into a blender or food processor with the curd cheese. Purée until smooth, then add the basil leaves (removing any coarse bits of stalk), the Worcestershire sauce and seasoning. Whizz again in the machine, then taste, adjusting the seasoning as necessary. Pour into individual soup bowls and chill until ready to serve, at which stage you can add a couple of ice cubes if you wish.

Serves 4

Avocado Soup

It is the addition of ground cumin which makes all the difference to this fairly basic soup.

METRIC/IMPERIAL	AMERICAN
2 large ripe avocados	2 large ripe avocados

2 *cloves garlic*
3 *tablespoons lemon juice*
1½ *teaspoons ground cumin*
600 *ml/1 pint half cream (or use equal quantities milk and single cream)*
salt and freshly milled black pepper
To garnish:
4 *tablespoons chopped chives*

2 *cloves garlic*
3 *tablespoons lemon juice*
1½ *teaspoons ground cumin*
2½ *cups half cream (or use equal quantities milk and light cream)*
salt and freshly milled black pepper
To garnish:
4 *tablespoons chopped chives*

Halve the avocados, remove the stones and peel them. Crush the garlic. Place the avocado flesh in a blender or food processor with the garlic, lemon juice and ground cumin. Purée until smooth, then, keeping the motor running, pour in the cream in a steady stream. Season to taste with salt and plenty of freshly milled black pepper. Pour into a serving dish, add the stones (this helps to preserve the colour of the soup), cover with clingwrap and chill for at least two hours. Sprinkle with the chives before serving.

Serves 4

Iced Clam Soup

Clams are not easy to open, but it is not an impossible task. Ideally use an oyster knife, or one with a strong short blade, but if it has a point to it, I would strongly suggest that you wear a pair of gardening or similar gloves, so that if your hand slips you will not cut yourself. Insert the knife at the hinge end and then prize it open.

METRIC/IMPERIAL
10 *large fresh clams*
1 *small onion*

AMERICAN
10 *large fresh clams*
1 *small onion*

300 ml/½ pint single cream
150 ml/¼ pint milk
juice of 1 lemon
salt and freshly milled black
    pepper
To garnish:
few ice cubes
2 tablespoons chopped parsley

1¼ cups light cream
⅝ cup milk
juice of 1 lemon
salt and freshly milled black
    pepper
To garnish:
few ice cubes
2 tablespoons chopped parsley

Open the clams (see above). Peel the onion. Put all the ingredients into a blender or food processor and process at high speed until smooth. Turn into a serving bowl and chill for two hours. Just before serving, drop a few ice cubes into the bowl and sprinkle with the parsley.

Serves 4

Iced Cucumber Soup

There are endless permutations of this soup made throughout the Middle East, some using only yogurt and cucumber and no cream, others using a higher proportion of yogurt to cucumber, but this is undoubtedly one of my favourite versions.

METRIC/IMPERIAL
1 large cucumber
1 clove of garlic
300 ml/½ pint single cream
150 ml/¼ pint natural yogurt
2 tablespoons wine vinegar
salt and freshly milled black
    pepper
2 tablespoons chopped mint
To garnish:
sprigs of fresh mint

AMERICAN
1 large cucumber
1 clove of garlic
1¼ cups light cream
⅝ cup natural yogurt
2 tablespoons wine vinegar
salt and freshly milled black
    pepper
2 tablespoons chopped mint
To garnish:
sprigs of fresh mint

Wipe the cucumber, but do not peel it. Grate it coarsely into a bowl. Crush the garlic and add to the cucumber together with the cream, yogurt, vinegar, seasoning and mint. Turn into a serving bowl and chill in the refrigerator for at least one hour. Taste and adjust the seasoning when the flavours have infused and garnish with sprigs of mint before serving.

Serves4–6

Kashmiri Yogurt Soup

This refreshing soup is given a distinctively Indian taste by the addition of ground cumin and chopped coriander.

METRIC/IMPERIAL	AMERICAN
½ large cucumber	½ large cucumber
½ teaspoon salt	½ teaspoon salt
450 ml/¾ pint natural yogurt	2 cups natural yogurt
150 ml/¼ pint milk	⅝ cup milk
1 clove garlic, crushed	1 clove garlic, crushed
1 tablespoon olive oil	1 tablespoon olive oil
2 teaspoons white wine vinegar	2 teaspoons white wine vinegar
1 teaspoon ground cumin	1 teaspoon ground cumin
1 tablespoon chopped coriander	1 tablespoon chopped coriander
freshly milled black pepper	freshly milled black pepper

Dice the cucumber finely. Put into a colander, sprinkle with the salt and leave to drain for 30 minutes. Turn the yogurt into a bowl then stir in the milk, garlic, olive oil, vinegar, cumin, coriander, and then finally the cucumber. Season to taste with a little extra salt, if necessary, and plenty of freshly milled black pepper. Chill for at least 30 minutes before serving, to allow the flavours to infuse.

Serves 4

Fresh Berry Soup

Fruit soups are a feature of both Balkan and Russian cuisine and are made with a variety of different fruits depending on the time of year; I had an excellent one during the cherry season in a pretty little restaurant in Budapest. They differ from sweet fruit purées in that they are always slightly sharp.

METRIC/IMPERIAL
450 g/1 lb fresh raspberries, blackberries, ripe gooseberries or blackcurrants
4 egg yolks
50–100 g/2–4 oz caster sugar (see method)
150 ml/¼ pint water
150 ml/¼ pint double cream
To garnish:
2 tablespoons chopped chives

AMERICAN
1 lb fresh raspberries, blackberries, ripe gooseberries or blackcurrants
4 egg yolks
¼–½ cup superfine sugar (see method)
⅝ cup of water
⅝ cup heavy cream
To garnish:
2 tablespoons chopped chives

Wash the berries and purée in a blender or food processor, then sieve them to remove all the pips. Blend the egg yolks with the sugar and a third of the fruit purée in the top of a double saucepan or in a bowl which can be placed over a pan of hot water. The amount of sugar will depend on the type and sweetness of the fruit, so add the minimum amount to start with and then add extra sugar after the cream has been added, if necessary.

Put the saucepan or bowl over a pan of gently simmering water and allow the mixture to thicken, stirring all the time. Remove from the heat and stir in the remaining fruit purée, the water and almost all the cream. Chill for at least six hours before serving as it should be very cold. Just before serving, spoon over the remaining cream to make a pattern and sprinkle with the chopped chives.

Serves 4

Curried Apple Soup

This is a marvellous soup for a hot summer's day, and should be served really well chilled.

METRIC/IMPERIAL
300 ml/½ pint natural yogurt
1 tablespoon garam masala
600 ml/1 pint unsweetened apple
  juice
2 tablespoons finely chopped
  coriander
salt and freshly milled black
  pepper

AMERICAN
1½ cups natural yogurt
1 tablespoon garam masala
2½ cups unsweetened apple juice
2 tablespoons finely chopped
  coriander
salt and freshly milled black
  pepper

Turn the yogurt into a bowl and stir in the garam masala. Gradually whisk in the apple juice, then half the coriander. Season to taste with a little salt, if wished, and some freshly milled black pepper. Turn into a serving dish and chill for at least two hours. Sprinkle with the remaining coriander before serving.

Serves 4

Melon Soup

This soup looks very pretty if it is served in little glass bowls, rather than more traditional soup dishes. You may be surprised that the melon does not yield a very large quantity of pulp, but I can assure you that it is very filling.

METRIC/IMPERIAL
1 large, ripe honeydew melon
juice 1 lemon

AMERICAN
1 large, ripe honeydew melon
juice 1 lemon

scant ¼ teaspoon ground cinnamon	scant ¼ teaspoon ground cinnamon
8 ice cubes	8 ice cubes
To garnish:	To garnish:
sprigs of mint	sprigs of mint

Halve the melon and remove the seeds. Scoop out the flesh with a dessertspoon and put into a blender or food processor. Whizz until smooth, then add the lemon juice and cinnamon and whizz again. Divide between four serving dishes and chill for about an hour.

Just before serving, put two ice cubes into each bowl and decorate with sprigs of mint.

Serves 4

Fresh Tomato Juice

In order to make really good fresh tomato juice you do need to use tomatoes with plenty of flavour, or you will end up with something that tastes very insipid. If it is the first time you have tried making it, you may also be surprised that it is not the dark red of commercially produced juices – these usually contain some concentrated tomato purée.

METRIC/IMPERIAL	AMERICAN
450 g/1 lb tomatoes	1 lb tomatoes
½ teaspoon sugar	½ teaspoon sugar
salt and freshly milled black pepper	salt and freshly milled black pepper
few drops Worcestershire sauce (optional)	few drops of Worcestershire sauce (optional)

Very roughly chop the tomatoes and put into a blender or food processor. Whizz until they are very smooth, then sieve to remove all the pips and the skin. Add the sugar and season to taste with salt, pepper and a little Worcestershire sauce if liked. Pour into glasses and add a couple of ice cubes to each one.

Serves 2–3

Mixed Vegetable Cocktail

This cocktail is best if served well chilled, so if you wish to serve it immediately, replace the water with crushed ice before puréeing.

METRIC/IMPERIAL	AMERICAN
2 carrots	2 carrots
2 tomatoes	2 tomatoes
2 small sticks celery	2 small sticks celery
4–6 sprigs of parsley	4–6 sprigs of parsley
salt and freshly milled black pepper	salt and freshly milled black pepper
juice of a lemon	juice of a lemon
350 ml/½ pint water	1¼ cups water
2 teaspoons yeast extract	2 teaspoon yeast extract

Peel the carrot and tomato and chop roughly with the celery. Put into a blender or food processor with all the remaining ingredients and whizz until smooth. Taste and adjust the seasoning, then chill.

Serves 2–4

Tomato Ice Cream

This makes an interesting starter, but it must be served when it is only half-frozen or it is too difficult to eat, as the high water content

31

in the tomatoes makes it freeze much harder than a more traditional sweet ice cream. I found that it therefore needed to be left in the refrigerator for a good hour before serving, or for 30 minutes at room temperature.

METRIC/IMPERIAL	AMERICAN
450 g/1 lb tomatoes	1 lb tomatoes
a pinch of sugar	a pinch of sugar
2 teaspoons chilli sauce	2 teaspoons chilli sauce
2 slightly rounded tablespoons chopped dill or basil	2 slightly rounded tablespoons chopped dill or basil
1 green pepper	1 green pepper
150 ml/¼ pint double cream	⅝ cup heavy cream
salt and freshly milled black pepper	salt and freshly milled black pepper

Roughly chop the tomatoes and put them into a blender or processor. Purée until smooth, then sieve into a bowl. Add the sugar, chilli sauce and dill or basil. De-seed the pepper and chop finely. Add to the tomato juice. Lightly whip the cream until it holds its shape, then fold in the tomato mixture. Season to taste with salt and pepper

Place in a freezer and freeze for about one hour or until it is just beginning to form crystals round the edge. Remove from the freezer and beat well. Replace in the freezer and re-freeze for about another 30 minutes, then remove from the freezer and beat well. Pile the mixture into four ramekins and freeze for about four hours or until quite firm. If wishing to store the ramekins for more than about two hours in the freezer, keep covered with a double layer of clingwrap. Allow to defrost (as above), before serving.

Serves 4 as a starter

Tomato Water Ice

The celebrated actor, James Robertson-Justice – a man who was exceedingly fond of this food – gave me this recipe of his 20 years ago.

METRIC/IMPERIAL	AMERICAN
900 g/2 lb tomatoes	*2 lb ripe tomatoes*
1 small onion	*1 small onion*
3 sprigs marjoram	*3 sprigs marjoram*
juice of 1 lemon	*juice of 1 lemon*
salt and freshly milled black pepper	*salt and freshly milled black pepper*
2 teaspoons sugar (see below)	*2 teaspoons sugar (see below)*
To garnish:	To garnish:
sprigs of mint	*sprigs of mint*

Chop the tomatoes roughly. Peel and halve the onion. Put the tomatoes, onion, marjoram and lemon juice into a blender or food processor and purée until smooth. Season with salt and pepper and add sugar to taste – the amount required will depend on the sweetness of the tomatoes. Sieve into a freezing container and freeze for four hours or until solid.

Remove from the freezer and leave at room temperature for about 15 minutes before serving, or in the fridge for 30–45 minutes. Turn out of the container on to a piece of waxed or non-stick paper and crush the ice with a rolling pin. Pile the crystals into individual glasses, garnish with mint and serve as soon as possible.

Serves 4

Tomato Jelly with Aioli

If you wish, you can be painstaking about this and make your own tomato juice (see page 30), but I have made it with both fresh and canned, and quite honestly the difference, unless you are lucky enough to find some really superbly-flavoured tomatoes (and they do still exist), is quite honestly very little.

METRIC/IMPERIAL
For the tomato jelly:
600 ml/1 pint tomato juice
15 g/½ oz or 1 envelope powdered
  gelatine
2 teaspoons Worcestershire sauce
1 tablespoon lemon juice
salt and freshly milled black
  pepper
1 green pepper
150 ml/¼ pint aioli (page 16)

AMERICAN
For the tomato jelly:
2½ cups tomato juice
1 envelope unflavoured gelatin
2 teaspoons Worcestershire sauce
1 tablespoon lemon juice
salt and freshly milled black
  pepper
1 green pepper
⅝ cup aioli (page 16)

Pour four tablespoons of the tomato juice into a small basin. Sprinkle over the gelatine (gelatin) and leave to soften for five minutes. Stand over a pan of hot water and leave until the gelatine has completely dissolved, then add to the remainder of the tomato juice with the Worcestershire sauce and lemon juice. Season well with salt, if necessary, and plenty of black pepper, remembering that as the jelly chills down the flavours become less pronounced. Put on one side until it is beginning to set. Dice the pepper, discarding the core and seeds and stir into the jelly when it is beginning to set. Pour into a wetted 600 ml/1 pint mould and chill for at least two hours or until set.

To serve the jelly, dip the mould quickly into some very hot water, then invert onto a serving dish. Serve with the aioli.

Serves 6 as a starter or 4 as a main course with salad.

FISH

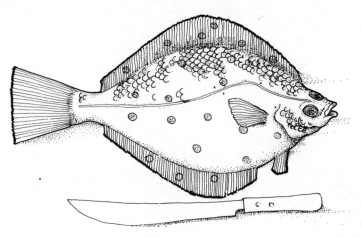

There are a number of different ways in which fish can be eaten raw and all of them – with the exception of shellfish such as oysters and sea urchins, and fresh raw fish served like Japanese sashimi – are age-old methods of preservation.

Even if you are going to cook fish it is important that it is fresh, but it is absolutely essential if you plan to eat it raw. You therefore must be certain that you are using a reputable fishmonger. Certainly, if you see any Japanese in a fishmonger's queue, you can be fairly sure that the fish will be fresh. If you are in any doubt at all though, inform the fishmonger, as another safeguard, that you are going to eat it raw. Should you not have a good fishmonger, the next best thing is to use frozen fish from a reliable source as this is usually frozen on the fishing vessel within hours of being caught, and freezing will also help to destroy any bacteria or other organisms that might be present.

To be sure that shellfish are fresh they must be alive when you open them. For molluscs (those with two hinged shells, like oysters and mussels), which are most commonly eaten raw, this is not difficult to check as if the fish is alive the shell will be tightly closed. If it is open, tap it sharply, or plunge it into cold water. If it closes up the fish is alive, but if it does not, discard it immediately.

Fresh Fish and Shellfish

The best known fresh raw fish dish is undoubtedly sashimi. I have not given an actual recipe for this, as it only consists of strips of skinned fish fillet, served with a combination of soy sauce and Japanese horseradish (wasabi). What is most remarkable about sashimi is the way in which the Japanese arrange it. One, or a mixture of fish can be used, but it is arranged exquisitely, often beautifully set off by atttractive lacquered plates. Various designs are wrought with the strips of fish in intricate patterns, from fans to fish shapes. The dish is then garnished with leaves and flower buds.

Almost any fish can be used for sashimi, although I would advise against using scavenging fish such as mackerel or trout (and other freshwater fish) that have not been farmed, as there is always a greater risk of these fish containing 'foreign bodies'. They can be used perfectly well, however, if pickled or cured, although one should use a slightly larger quantity of salt than if curing salmon, for example.

Another way of eating fish raw, now being served in some of the nouvelle cuisine restaurants, is fish tartare. The raw, filleted and skinned fish is lightly flaked and mixed with a little seasoning and lemon juice or vinegar. It can either be rolled into balls or arranged on plates, and is usually served with a cream and herb-based sauce, or even just simple whipped or soured cream, or crème fraiche flavoured with herbs.

When it comes to eating shellfish raw it is generally the molluscs, rather than the crustaceans such as lobsters, which are eaten raw. The most common fish to be eaten in this way is, of course, the oyster, but mussels (often referred to as the poor man's oyster), clams, cockles, winkles and even whelks can all be used as well. Sea urchins are also a great delicacy, especially the corals, but as they are covered with very sharp spines, you must wear stout gloves, both to gather them and to hold them, before cutting in half with a sharp knife.

Salted and Cured Fish

The best known salted fish is probably the anchovy, a native of the English Channel and the Mediterranean, and a member of the herring family. Although it is possible to buy fresh anchovies, because they deteriorate rapidly (especially in the heat of the Mediterranean) they have traditionally always been salted. At one time one could buy salted anchovies, in barrels, but this is becoming an increasingly rare sight, so one has to make do with those preserved either in brine or canned in oil.

Salt herrings were also sold in the same way, and, until recently I could buy them from a Jewish delicatessen in London's Soho. Now, however, they tell me that there is no longer any demand, so they have ceased to stock them. However, if you do find any, salt herrings should be soaked in cold water or milk for 12–24 hours, while salted anchovies should be soaked for a minimum of two hours.

In Holland where maatjes pickled herrings (so called because they only use the young female herrings and *maatjes* is the Dutch for virgin) they also eat what they call 'green herrings'. These are fresh raw herrings which are very lightly salted and appear in the markets, shops and restaurants from the beginning of May, at the start of the new herring season.

But undoubtedly the 'king' of salted fish must be caviare, a word that is synonymous with that of millionaire. One does have to be just about in that bracket to be able to afford the Beluga or Sevruga varieties. I have been lucky enough to eat it on a few occasions by courtesy of some very generous friends.

Lumpfish roe is always referred to as the poor man's caviare, and certainly it cannot compare in any way to the real thing. It is not however to be despised as it makes a very attractive garnish, as well as giving flavour to a number of dishes. In fact a closer resemblance to the genuine article is possibly the recipe on page 41 for Fresh Salmon Caviare.

Curing fish with fresh herbs and a small quantity of salt, which destroys any bacteria but does not have the effect of long term preservation, is becoming increasingly popular. It is extremely simple to do at home and seems to bring out all the natural flavour of the fish. There is also the added advantage that as only a small quantity of salt is used, it should not offend the 'anti-sodium' lobby.

Many people prefer salmon cured in this way to smoked salmon, but any fish can be used. Although dill is the most usual herb, there is no reason why chives, tarragon, basil or chervil cannot replace it.

What is important is that it does not have a flavour that is too overpowering: thyme and rosemary would not really be suitable.

Pickled Fish

It is fascinating to observe how, although using different ingredients, an almost identical method of preserving fish exists in Northern Europe and in South America. In Northern Europe the fish most commonly pickled was that which was most easily caught, namely the herring from the North Sea which was preserved in vinegar.

Using exactly the same principle of preserving food with acid, throughout South America, the neighbouring Caribbean and even the Pacific Islands, fish has for centuries been steeped in citrus juices, usually lime or lemon juice, which was their most readily available form of edible acid. The main difference between the two methods is that vinegar is a long term method of preservation, while steeping in citrus juice will only preserve the fish for a few days as there is a higher water content and lower acidic content in citrus juice than in vinegar.

The problems of over-fishing of herring in the 1970s resulted in a decline in popularity of the pickled herring in the United Kingdom, although, its various forms – some are lightly salted, others have spiced vinegar added, and some have a definite sweet/sour flavour – are still extremely popular throughout Scandinavia, Germany and Holland. However, at the same time as the traditional pickled herring has lost favour, the method of pickling in citrus juice has gained popularity. One reason for this may be that pickling fish in vinegar leaves a distinct 'vinegary' taste, whereas fish that has been steeped in citrus juice only retains a slight hint of the preserving liquor and has a much more delicate flavour, which fits in with modern eating trends.

Once the fish has been pickled, it can then be used in a number of ways. It can be eaten just on its own with a little French dressing spooned over the top; a variety of other ingredients such as herbs, spices, vegetables and fruit can all be added; and they are always excellent served in a light cream or soured cream sauce.

Smoked Fish

Smoking is one of the oldest methods of preservation: wood smoke sterilizes meat and fish. Evidence has been found that the Larnians, an ancient Irish tribe, were smoking salmon 4,000 years ago, although they are unlikely to have produced anything quite as delectable as we can eat today!

There are two methods of smoking fish: cold smoking, when the temperature does not rise above 15°C/60°F; and hot smoking, when the fish is placed closer to a hotter fire so that it becomes cooked in the process. Salmon is the fish one instinctively thinks of when talking about cold smoked fish and it is certainly one of the most delicious. All food that is smoked is first salted, and in the case of salmon smoking this is a particularly skilled process. Some curers use only salt or brine, while others add spices such as juniper berries as well. Every salmon smoker has his own particular way of smoking and curing the fish, but it is generally true to say that a London cure has a lower salt level and is generally milder in flavour than a Scottish cure.

Smoked salmon is still considered to be a luxury, and while it would perhaps be rather sad if it were ever to be considered to be as mundane as a smoked mackerel, the increasing amount of farmed Scottish salmon has made it more readily available and helped to keep the price at a steady level.

Kippers are another fish which are cold smoked, and they can often be used as a substitute for smoked salmon, as although they are more frequently eaten cooked, they are delicious just as they are. The greatest problem these days is finding a good kipper as some of them have not ever seen any smoke and are injected with 'smokey' flavour. If you are buying them loose from a fishmonger they should be all right, and you may be lucky enough to find them uncoloured. If they are pre-packed, read what they contain very carefully. A proper kipper should only be herring and salt – and preferably not too great a proportion of the latter.

Smoked cod's roe is another fish which is sometimes injected rather than being properly smoked, possibly because it is difficult to do well, and injecting is an easy option. You want to choose a roe that is orangey-brown in colour rather than the vivid pink one sees all too frequently.

There are other fish (as well as cod and haddock which are usually cooked after smoking) which are sometimes cold-smoked as well. One can buy 'kippered' mackerel from time to time and trout fillets are sometims cold smoked, especially the pink-fleshed variety. I have also seen brill smoked, and the contrast on a platter of pink-fleshed salmon and golden/beige brill is extremely attractive.

Salmon Tartare

When a friend of mine raved about the salmon tartare he had eaten in a restaurant, he also added that according to the chef, it was essential that it was made with three types of salmon: fresh, smoked, and Gravad Lax. However, as I thought it was unlikely that many households would happen to have some spare Gravad Lax in the fridge and that not many shops actually sell it, I have adapted the recipe slightly so that it uses only fresh and smoked salmon, but it is served with a dill-flavoured sauce.

METRIC/IMPERIAL
450 g/1 lb fresh salmon
175 g/6 oz smoked salmon or use
   good quality smoked salmon
   pieces
salt and freshly milled black
   pepper
2 tablespoons tarragon vinegar
sprigs of fresh dill
For the sauce:
150 ml/¼ pint soured cream
½ teaspoon sugar
2 tablespoons chopped dill
1 tablespoon chopped chives
salt and freshly milled black
   pepper

AMERICAN
1 lb fresh salmon
6 oz smoked salmon or use good
   quality smoked salmon pieces
salt and freshly milled black
   pepper
2 tablespoons tarragon vinegar
sprigs of fresh dill
For the sauce:
⅝ cup sour cream
½ teaspoon sugar
2 tablespoons chopped dill
1 tablespoon chopped chives
salt and freshly milled black
   pepper

40

Skin and bone the salmon – at this stage you should be left with about 375 g/12 oz. Using a fork, gently mash the flesh of the fish, then turn into a bowl. Do the same with the smoked salmon, but you may find it easier to do this with two forks, so that you just tear it apart. Add to the fresh salmon. Add the vinegar and seasoning and mix lightly together. Divide the mixture into four and arrange on individual serving plates, garnished with the fresh dill.

Blend together all the ingredients for the sauce and serve this sauce separately with the salmon, so that everyone can just mix in as much fish to sauce as they wish.

Serves 4

Fresh Salmon Caviare

This recipe was given to me by one of the many Japanese ladies who frequent my local fishmonger. Although you can salt the roe whole, she suggested that it is even better if you first remove the outer skin and place the skinned roe into a basin. This, however, is not as easy as it may first appear, as it is actually quite difficult to pull off the skin without squashing the eggs. The best way is to put the roe on a board with the skin on the bottom, then using a small, sharp knife, slice along parallel with the board, as if you were skinning a fillet of fish. Then turn the roe over and repeat on the other side.

METRIC/IMPERIAL
100 g/4 oz fresh salmon roe
scant 2.5 ml/½ teaspoon salt
freshly milled black pepper
To serve:
1 lemon or lime

AMERICAN
4 oz fresh salmon roe
scant ½ teaspoon salt
freshly milled black pepper
To serve:
1 lemon or lime

Skin the roe as above and put into a basin with the salt and pepper. Cover with clingwrap and leave for 24 hours. Stir lightly, then turn into a small serving dish, or arrange on individual plates. Cut the lemon or lime into wedges and serve these with the roe, together with thin slices of hot toast.

Serves 4 as a starter

Caviare Mousse

Well, not actually, and indeed it would be sacrilege to do such a thing with the genuine article: but this is lumpfish roe mousse. You can also buy caviare-type salmon roe, and I think this would be even better for this recipe as it would be a prettier colour.

METRIC/IMPERIAL
150 g/½ oz or 1 envelope
   powdered gelatine
4 tablespoons water
300 ml/½ pint soured cream
2 eggs, separated
juice ½ a lemon
1 tablespoon mayonnaise (page
   6)
1 teaspoon Worcestershire sauce
100 g/4 oz lumpfish or salmon roe
salt and freshly milled black
   pepper
To garnish:
slices of cucumber
slices of lemon

AMERICAN
1 envelope unflavoured gelatin
4 tablespoons water
1¼ cups sour cream
2 eggs, separated
juice ½ a lemon
1 tablespoon mayonnaise (page
   6)
1 teaspoon Worcestershire sauce
4 oz lumpfish or salmon roe
salt and freshly milled black
   pepper
To garnish:
slices of cucumber
slices of lemon

Sprinkle the gelatine (gelatin) over the water in a basin or cup and leave to soften for five minutes, then stand over a pan of gently simmering water until it has dissolved. Blend the cream with the egg yolks, lemon juice, mayonnaise and Worcestershire sauce, and beat well. Stir in the lumpfish roe, then the dissolved gelatine, season to taste. Put on one side until the mixture is beginning to set. Whisk the egg whites until stiff, then fold into the caviare mixture.

Divide between six ramekins, then chill for at least one hour or until set. Garnish each ramekin with two slices of cucumber and a slice of lemon, twisted together to form a butterfly.

Serves 6 as a starter

Gravad Lax

This Swedish speciality which is traditionally served at the feast of Midsummer's Day, is undoubtedly the best known and most popular of all the cured fish. As well as making it with fresh wild salmon, I have made it with farmed salmon, salmon trout and the large, pink-fleshed farmed rainbow trout as well.

METRIC/IMPERIAL
650 g/1 ½ lb salmon tailpiece
1 teaspoon black peppercorns
1 heaped tablespoon sea salt
1 heaped tablespoon granulated
   sugar
1 tablespoon brandy
1 heaped tablespoon chopped dill
sprigs of fresh dill
For the sauce:
2 tablespoons French or German
   mustard
1 heaped tablespoon granulated
   sugar
1 large egg yolk
6 tablespoons olive oil
2 tablespoons white wine vinegar
1 heaped teaspoon chopped dill
salt and freshly milled black
   pepper

AMERICAN
1 ½ lb salmon tailpiece
1 teaspoon black peppercorns
1 heaped tablespoon sea salt
1 heaped tablespoon caster sugar
1 tablespoon brandy
1 heaped tablespoon chopped dill
sprigs of fresh dill
For the sauce:
2 tablespoons French or German
   mustard
1 heaped tablespoon caster sugar
1 large egg yolk
6 tablespoon olive oil
2 tablespoons white wine vinegar
1 heaped teaspoon chopped dill
salt and freshly ground black
   pepper

Fillet the fish into two triangles, or ask the fishmonger to do this for you. Coarsely crush the peppercorns and mix with the sea salt, sugar, brandy and dill. Spread a quarter of this over the base of a dish or tray. Lay one of the pieces of salmon skin side down on top of the mixture and spread half of the remaining pickle on the cut side. Place the other piece of salmon, skin side up, over the first. Rub the remainder of the pickled mixture well into the skin.

Cover all over with clingwrap, then place a board or second plate on top and weight it down. Leave in the fridge for at least 12 hours, but for up to five days, turning the salmon once a day. To serve, cut the salmon into thin slices and arrange on a serving platter. Garnish with sprigs of dill.

To make the sauce, beat the mustard with the sugar and egg yolk until it is smooth. Gradually add the oil and vinegar, a teaspoon at a time, beating well. Add the chopped dill and season to taste with salt and pepper. Serve this sauce separately with the salmon.

Serves 6

Cured Plaice (Flounder) with Wasabi

Japanese wasabi powder is a mixture of Japanese horseradish and mustard, which when mixed with milk or water makes a bright green paste. It is very hot, so you only require a very little of it.

METRIC/IMPERIAL	AMERICAN
2 plaice fillets, weighing about 225 g/8 oz each	2 flounder fillets, weighing about 8 oz each
1 teaspoon coarsely ground pepper	1 teaspoon coarsely ground black pepper
1 teaspoon chopped dill	1 teaspoon chopped dill
1 teaspoon fine sea salt	1 teaspoon fine sea salt
1 teaspoon sugar	1 teaspoon sugar
2 tablespoons lime juice	

2 tablespoons olive oil
1 tablespoon sesame oil
1 tablespoon Japanese wasabi
 powder
about 3 teaspoons milk
To garnish:
tomato skins

2 tablespoons lime juice
2 tablespoons olive oil
1 tablespoon sesame oil
1 tablespoon Japanese wasabi
 powder
about 3 teaspoons milk
To garnish:
tomato skins

Skin the fillets of fish. Mix together the pepper, dill, salt and sugar. Sprinkle half of this over a plate large enough to hold both the fillets. Lay the fillets on top, then scatter over the remaining curing mixture. Sprinkle with one tablespoon of the lime juice and one tablespoon of the olive oil. Cover with clingwrap and marinate for 24 to 36 hours, turning the fish two or three times.

Lift the fillets out of the curing mixture, cut into thin slices and arrange on a serving plate. Mix together the remaining lime juice and olive oil, together with the sesame oil. Brush this mixture all over the fish. Garnish the fish with tomato roses, made by rolling a continuous spiral of the tomato skin.

Blend the wasabi powder with the milk to make a paste and serve this sauce, in a tiny dish, separately with the fish.

Serves 4 as a starter

Marinated Mackerel with Tarragon

Dill weed is the herb most commonly used for curing fish, but there is no reason at all why other herbs cannot be used and tarragon, which teams so well with fish, is a particularly good one to use. It is important with fish like mackerel and trout to use a high proportion of salt during curing to ensure that any small organisms that might be in it are killed.

METRIC/IMPERIAL	AMERICAN
2 *mackerel, weighing about 450 g/1 lb each*	2 *mackerel weighing about 1 lb each*
4 *tablespoons fine sea salt*	4 *tablespoons fine sea salt*
4 *tablespoons caster sugar*	4 *tablespoons superfine sugar*
3 *tablespoons chopped tarragon*	3 *tablespoons chopped tarragon*
To garnish:	To garnish:
sprigs of fresh tarragon	*sprigs of fresh tarragon*
For the sauce:	For the sauce:
2 *tablespoons French mustard*	2 *tablespoons French mustard*
2 *teaspoons clear honey*	2 *teaspoons clear honey*
1 *tablespoon lemon juice*	1 *tablespoon lemon juice*
3 *tablespoons olive oil*	3 *tablespoons olive oil*
1 *tablespoon chopped chives*	1 *tablespoon chopped chives*

Either ask your fishmonger to gut and fillet the fish, or do this yourself, but make sure they are thoroughly washed after gutting. Trim away the inside of the belly cavity. Mix together the salt, sugar and tarragon. Sprinkle a third of it in a dish large enough to hold the two fish. Lay two fillets on top, skin side down, scatter over another third of the curing mixture, then lay the remaining fillets on top, with the skin side up, so that the fish are re-assembled to their natural state. Sprinkle the remaining curing mixture over the top.

Cover the whole dish with clingwrap, then place a board or plate on top and some weights. Place in the fridge and leave to marinate for 36 to 48 hours, turning the fish several times in the marinade.

Lift the fillets out of the curing mixture, wipe off the surplus marinade and cut the flesh into neat strips away from the skin, as if you were slicing smoked salmon. Arrange on a large serving platter and garnish with sprigs of fresh tarragon.

To make the sauce, spoon the mustard into a basin. Add the honey, then stir in the lemon juice. Gradually stir in the oil, then stir in the chives. Turn into a jug and serve separately with the fish.

Serves 6–8 as a starter, 4 as a main course.

Pickled Herrings

This is a basic recipe for pickled herrings, which can be varied in any number of ways, and can indeed be used for other fish such as mackerel and trout.

You can add a tablespoon of sugar to the vinegar, which will give the fish a slight sweet/sour flavour, or other spices can be added such as allspice, coriander, dill, or fennel seed, as well as fresh herbs such as dill and tarragon.

It is worth doing a minimum of six fish at any one time as they can be stored in a cool place for several months.

METRIC/IMPERIAL	AMERICAN
6 herrings	6 herrings
50 g/2 oz salt	¼ cup salt
600 ml/1 pint water	2½ cups water
1 large onion	1 large onion
600 ml/1 pint distilled malt or cider vinegar	2½ cups distilled malt or cider vinegar
1 tablespoon mixed pickling spice	1 tablespoon mixed pickling spice
1 dried chilli pepper	1 dried chilli pepper
1 bay leaf	1 bay leaf

Clean and bone the herrings, or ask the fishmonger to do this for you. Dissolve the salt in the water, add the herrings and leave for two hours. Drain, rinse in cold water and dry well.

Peel and thinly slice the onion. Roll up each herring, skin side outside, with a few pieces of onion in each. Secure with a cocktail stick and pack into a wide-necked jar.

While the herrings are brining, put the vinegar and pickling spice into a pan. Bring slowly to the boil, then remove from the heat and leave for 30 minutes. Strain and cool. Pour the cooled vinegar over the herrings in the jar and add the chilli and bay leaf. Cover the jar tightly and leave in a cool place for six days before using.

Scandinavian Herring Salad

Endless variations of this are served throughout Scandinavia and Germany. As well as using different vegetables such as cucumbers, dill pickles and beetroot, you can use any variety of pickled herring you like – I personally prefer one of the ones with just a little sugar added to it.

METRIC/IMPERIAL
8 small fillets pickled herring
1 small onion
1 dessert apple
2 teaspoons lemon juice
150 ml/¼ pint soured cream
1 tablespoon chopped dill
salt and freshly milled black
 pepper

AMERICAN
8 small fillets pickled herring
1 small onion
1 dessert apple
2 teaspoons lemon juice
⅝ cup sour cream
1 tablespoon chopped dill
salt and freshly milled black
 pepper

Drain the herrings and cut into bite-sized pieces. Put into a bowl. Peel the onion and slice finely into rings. Core and slice the unpeeled apple and sprinkle with the lemon juice. Put the onion and apple into the basin with the herring. Add the cream, seasoning and dill and blend the mixture together. Season to taste with a little salt and plenty of freshly milled black pepper, then turn into a serving dish.

Serves 4

Kokoda

A speciality of the Pacific islands, in which the macerated fish is served in a piquant coconut cream. Although you can use any firm-fleshed fish (monkfish would be ideal) it is superb made with fresh tuna if you can get hold of some.

METRIC/IMPERIAL	AMERICAN
650 g/1½ lb firm-fleshed fish (see above)	1½ lb firm-fleshed fish (see above)
6 tablespoons lime or lemon juice	6 tablespoons lime or lemon juice
For the sauce:	For the sauce:
2 coconuts	2 coconuts
1 lemon	1 lemon
1 small onion	1 small onion
1 green chilli	1 green chilli
1 teaspoon salt	1 teaspoon salt
150 ml/¼ pint water	⅝ cup water
To garnish:	To garnish:
1 lemon or lime	1 lemon or lime

Remove any bones and skin from the fish and cut into 1.25 cm/½ inch cubes. Put into a shallow dish, pour over the lime or lemon juice and leave to macerate for at least four hours or overnight.

Crack open the cocunuts, pour off the milk and grate the flesh. Put into a bowl. Finely grate the lemon rind and squeeze the juice. Peel and finely chop the onion, and finely chop the chilli, discarding all the seeds. Add the lemon rind and juice, onion, chilli, salt and water to the coconut flesh. Mix well and squeeze out the cream with your hands; if, like many people you are at all allergic to chillies, do this with rubber gloves on.

Strain the coconut cream through a piece of muslin and chill while the fish is macerating.

Strain off the liquid from the fish and arrange the cubes of fish in six individual serving dishes. Spoon over the coconut cream, cut the lemon or lime into slices and use to garnish the dish.

Serves 6

Scallops with Basil Cream

For this recipe it is not necessary to buy the large, expensive scallops, as it can be made just as well with the smaller Queens.

These should not be cut into pieces, but are best left whole.

METRIC/IMPERIAL	AMERICAN
225 g/8 oz scallops	8 oz scallops
juice 1½ lemons	juice 1½ lemons
freshly milled black pepper	freshly milled black pepper
100 ml/4 fl oz double cream	½ cup heavy cream
4 large sprigs basil	4 large sprigs basil
salt	salt

Remove any black veins from the scallops and, if large, cut into about four pieces, leaving the coral whole. Put into a basin with the lemon juice and pepper. Cover and leave for at least four to six hours, or overnight if wished. Stir in the double (heavy) cream. Coarsely chop the basil and add to the fish and lemon juice, stirring well. Taste and adjust the seasoning, then turn into a serving dish.

Serves 4 as a starter or 2–3 as a main course

Ceviche

Although I would not claim this to be the 'classic' recipe for Ceviche it is one that was given to me a few years ago by one of Mexico's most successful cookery writers.

METRIC/IMPERIAL	AMERICAN
675 g/1½ lb white fish fillets, e.g.	1½ lb white fish fillets, e.g.
haddock, cod, sole or halibut	haddock, cod, sole or halibut
1 medium-sized onion	1 medium-sized onion
juice 1 orange	juice 1 orange
juice 4 limes	juice 4 limes
4 ripe tomatoes	4 ripe tomatoes
1 small green pepper	1 small green pepper
4 tablespoons olive oil	4 tablespoons olive oil
1 tablespoon tomato purée	1 tablespoon tomato purée

1 teaspoon caster sugar	1 teaspoon superfine sugar
½ teaspoon Tabasco	½ teaspoon Tabasco
½ teaspoon dried oregano	½ teaspoon dried oregano
2 tablespoons chopped coriander	2 tablespoons chopped coriander
salt and freshly milled black pepper	salt and freshly milled black pepper
1 lettuce	1 lettuce

Skin the fish, cut into bite-sized pieces and place in a bowl. Finely chop the onion, add to the fish, then pour over the citrus juice. Cover and chill overnight, or for several hours until the fish has turned white and opaque, and looks like cooked fish.

Peel and chop the tomatoes and finely chop the pepper, discarding the core and seeds. Add to the fish with the olive oil, tomato purée, caster (superfine) sugar, Tabasco, oregano, and coriander. Season to taste with salt and pepper and leave to marinate for one hour for the flavour to infuse.

Shred the lettuce and arrange on individual serving dishes, then pile the fish on top, spooning over the sauce.

Serves 4

Celeriac with Smoked Salmon

A good way of stretching a small quantity of smoked salmon. It is nicest if it is left for about an hour or so before serving to allow the flavours to infuse.

METRIC/IMPERIAL	AMERICAN
150 ml/¼ pint mayonnaise (page 6)	⅝ cup mayonnaise (page 6)
150 ml/¼ pint soured cream	⅝ cup sour cream
1 tablespoon lemon juice	1 tablespoon lemon juice
1 rounded teaspoon French mustard	1 rounded teaspoon French mustard
1 celeriac, about 650g/1½ lb	1 celeriac about 1½ lb
	6 oz smoked salmon

175 g/6 oz smoked salmon
salt and freshly milled black pepper
To garnish (optional):
1 rounded tablespoon lumpfish roe
lemon wedges

salt and freshly milled black pepper
To garnish (optional):
1 rounded tablespoon lumpfish roe
lemon wedges

Blend the mayonnaise with the cream, lemon juice and mustard in a bowl. Peel the celeriac, then cut into matchstick pieces, adding the pieces to the mayonnaise mixture as soon as they are cut and stirring them in to prevent discolouration. Cut the smoked salmon into strips, add to the celeriac and mix well. Season with a little salt (the amount of salt needed will depend on how long you are preparing the salad before serving as the salt comes out of the salmon as the salad stands) and plenty of freshly milled black pepper. Mix well, then turn into a serving dish, cover with clingwrap and chill until shortly before serving.

If wished, garnish the top of the dish with the lumpfish roe and wedges of lemon.

Serves 4 as a main course, 6 as a starter

Smoked Salmon Mousse

This is really a cross between a pâté and a mousse: it is lighter than the usual fish pâté, but is not a 'set' mousse.

METRIC/IMPERIAL
100 g/4 oz smoked salmon pieces
100 g/4 oz curd cheese
juice of ½ lemon
150 ml/¼ pint soured cream
freshly milled black pepper
a pinch of cayenne pepper

AMERICAN
4 oz smoked salmon pieces
½ cup curd cheese
juice of ½ lemon
⅝ cup sour cream
freshly milled black pepper
a pinch of cayenne pepper

Put the smoked salmon pieces, curd cheese and lemon juice into a blender or food processor and whizz until smooth. Add the cream and whizz again, then season to taste with plenty of freshly milled black pepper and a pinch of cayenne. Turn into a serving dish and chill until ready to serve.

Serves 4

Smoked Salmon with Taramasalata

You want mild-cured smoked salmon for this, or you will find the end result rather salty.

METRIC/IMPERIAL	AMERICAN
2 rounded tablespoons whipped cream	2 rounded tablespoons whipped cream
50 g/2 oz taramasalata (see page 55)	2 oz taramasalata (see page 55)
4 slices smoked salmon, about 50 g/2 oz each	4 slices smoked salmon weighing about 2 oz each
7.5 cm/3 inch piece cucumber	3 inch piece cucumber
freshly milled black pepper	freshly milled black pepper
To garnish:	To garnish:
1 lemon	1 lemon
cress	cress

Fold the cream into the taramasalata. Lay one of the slices of salmon on a board and spread with a quarter of the taramasalata mixture. Cut the cucumber into four lengthways and lay a stick at one end of the salmon. Roll up, tucking in the sides of the salmon. Repeat this with the other three pieces of salmon. Arrange the salmon rolls on individual plates and grind over plenty of black pepper.

Cut the lemon into wedges and use to garnish the salmon with a little cress.

Serves 4 as a starter

Marinated Smoked Salmon

You do not need to use prime quality salmon for this recipe and, if you wish, you can even use pieces, although if doing this, make sure there is no skin and bones left on.

METRIC/IMPERIAL	AMERICAN
225 g/8 oz smoked salmon	8 oz smoked salmon
1 teaspoon green peppercorns	1 teaspoon green peppercorns
½ teaspoon dill seed	½ teaspoon dill seed
1 bay leaf	1 bay leaf
150 ml/¼ pint dry white wine	⅝ cup dry white wine
150 ml/¼ pint soured cream	⅝ cup sour cream
1 teaspoon French mustard	1 teaspoon French mustard
a pinch of salt	a pinch of salt
2 tablespoons lemon juice	2 tablespoons lemon juice

Place the salmon in a shallow dish. Sprinkle with the peppercorns and dill seed. Tear the bay leaf into several pieces, add to the dish and pour over the wine. Cover with clingwrap and leave for eight hours or overnight in the fridge.

Shortly before serving, remove the salmon from the marinade and arrange on a serving dish. Strain half the wine mixture into a basin and stir in the cream, mustard, salt and lemon juice. Season with extra black or green pepper, if necessary. Pour the sauce over the salmon.

Serves 4–6

Smoked Salmon and Horseradish Rolls

An excellent way of 'stretching' a small quantity of smoked salmon to make little appetisers for drinks or to serve as a starter. Obviously if fresh horseradish is available it would be preferable, in which case you will need to add a little vinegar.

METRIC/IMPERIAL	AMERICAN
100 g/4 oz curd cheese	½ cup curd cheese
2 tablespoons horseradish relish	2 tablespoons horseradish relish
25 g/1 oz shredded lettuce	½ cup shredded lettuce
salt and freshly milled black pepper	salt and freshly milled black pepper
100 g/4 oz smoked salmon	4 oz smoked salmon
a squeeze of lemon juice	a squeeze of lemon juice

Beat the cheese, then beat in the horseradish. Stir in the lettuce and season with a little salt and plenty of freshly milled black pepper. Cut the salmon into pieces about 4 × 3 inches/10 × 7.5 cm pieces. Divide the lettuce and horseradish mixture between them and roll up. Place on a serving dish, squeeze over some lemon juice and grind on some black pepper.

Makes about 12

Simple Taramasalata

Tarama is the Greek word for the dried and salted roe of the grey mullet, which is what this 'salad' should be made with. As this however, is not easily found outside of Greece and the Middle East, it has become more usual to make it with smoked cod's roe.

When buying smoked cod's roe, try to choose a roe that is a good orange colour, rather than a vivid pinky-red, which usually indicates that it has been dyed. It should also have a good, soft texture to it and not be hard and crumbly.

METRIC/IMPERIAL	AMERICAN
100 g/4 oz smoked cod's roe	4 oz smoked cod's roe

1 clove garlic	1 clove garlic
2 tablespoons lemon juice	2 tablespoons lemon juice
4 tablespoons olive oil	4 tablespoons olive oil
2 tablespoons cold water	2 tablespoons cold water
freshly milled black pepper	freshly milled black pepper

Remove the skin from the cod's roe and discard it. Crush the garlic. Pound the roe with the garlic and lemon juice until smooth; the quickest and easiest way to do this is in a blender or food processor. Gradually beat in the oil and water alternately until you have a thick, smooth purée. Season to taste with pepper.

Serves 4

Kipper and Mushroom Salad

A little chilli sauce in the dressing gives this salad a touch of piquance.

METRIC/IMPERIAL	AMERICAN
4 large kipper fillets	4 large kipper fillets
225 g/8 oz mushrooms	8 oz mushrooms
1 small red pepper	1 small red pepper
juice 1 lemon	juice 1 lemon
2 teaspoons chilli sauce	2 teaspoons chilli sauce
4 tablespoons single cream	4 tablespoons light cream
4 tablespoons olive oil	4 tablespoons olive oil
freshly milled black pepper	freshly milled black pepper
To garnish:	To garnish:
2 tablespoons chopped parsley	2 tablespoons chopped parsley

Skin the kipper fillets and cut them across the grain into thin strips about 0.75 cm/¼ inch wide. Put into a bowl. If the mushrooms are fairly large, slice them, if not just cut into halves or quarters. Core and de-seed the pepper, cut into strips and add to the kipper strips with the mushrooms.

Pour the lemon juice into a basin and, using a balloon, or similar whisk, whisk in the chilli sauce. Add the cream in a slow, steady stream, whisking all the time, then do the same with the olive oil. Season the dressing with plenty of freshly milled black pepper. Pour over the kippers, mushrooms and pepper and mix well.

Cover with clingwrap and chill for at least four hours, or overnight if wished. Remove the kippers, mushrooms and pepper from the bowl, using a draining spoon and arrange in a serving dish. Whisk the sauce (it tends to separate on standing) and pour over the salad. Sprinkle with the chopped parsley before serving.

Serves 4

Orange Marinated Kippers

In my first job, in a public relations company, we developed this recipe for the Herring Industry Board. It has remained a firm favourite of mine ever since.

METRIC/IMPERIAL	AMERICAN
2 tablespoons sunflower oil	2 tablespoons sunflower oil
grated rind and juice 1 orange	grated rind and juice 1 orange
6 black peppercorns	6 black peppercorns
3 small bay leaves	3 small bay leaves
8 small kipper fillets	8 small kipper fillets

Put the oil, orange rind and juice, peppercorns and bay leaves into a screw-topped jar and shake well. Skin the kipper fillets and lay them in a shallow dish. Pour over the orange marinade, cover with clingwrap and leave in the fridge for 12 to 24 hours.

Arrange the kipper fillets in a serving dish, strain over the marinade and serve with a tossed green salad.

Serves 4

Smoked Cod with Sherry

This has an interesting flavour and texture, but I think possibly one that should be reserved for raw fish enthusiasts.

METRIC/IMPERIAL
450 g/1 lb smoked cod fillet
5 tablespoons sweet sherry
1 tablespoon sesame oil
1 tablespoon lemon juice
1 small onion
freshly milled black pepper
1 red pepper
To garnish:
a few thin onion rings

AMERICAN
1 lb smoked cod fillet
5 tablespoons sweet sherry
1 tablespoon sesame oil
1 tablespoon lemon juice
1 small onion
freshly milled black pepper
1 red pepper
To garnish:
a few thin onion rings

Skin the cod, cut across the grain into thin strips, and place in a bowl. Mix the sherry with the oil and lemon juice, season with plenty of black pepper and pour over the fish. Finely chop the onion, add to the fish and mix lightly together. Cover and place in the refrigerator for at least four hours or overnight. Halve the pepper and discard the seeds, then cut into small dice and add to the fish. Arrange in a serving dish and garnish with a few onion rings.

Serves 4

MEAT

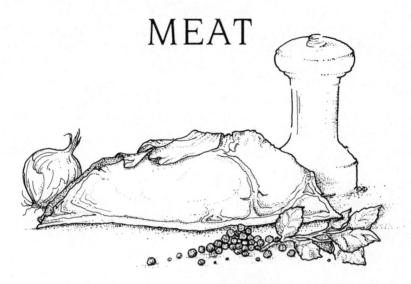

I am addicted to fresh raw meat, a habit which I notice my daughters acquired at a very early age: having taught them how to make home-made hamburgers, they frequently managed to demolish half the mixture before it ever got cooked. But in addition to tasting good, its nutritive value has long been recognised by many top-class atheletes. Rudolf Nureyev, for example, whose body had to be kept in perfect condition for years, ate it almost exclusively.

Steak tartare, is of course the best known raw meat dish, but this is far from being the only way in which one can eat meat raw. I am not convinced though that if you need to be persuaded into trying its delights, it is really the best one to start with. If you know how wonderful it tastes, the sight of that round patty of meat with a raw egg in the middle surrounded by little mounds of vegetables, sauces and herbs is glorious, but if you are a little dubious about the whole idea, the raw egg is probably the final thing to put you right off even trying it! I have therefore deliberately devised a couple of recipes in which the meat is formed into little balls, as I feel this makes a much better introduction to fresh raw meat.

For years there has been a popular misconception that if you are eating meat raw, certainly in the case of beef, that it has to be either fillet or best rump steak. This is absolute nonsense, as in most recipes the meat is ground, which breaks down its fibres. It is obviously essential, though, that really good quality, *fresh* meat is used, and I generally buy the best quality mince they have in the supermarket. Most good supermarkets throw away any minced meat that is not purchased at the end of the day, so you can be certain that such meat is very fresh.

It is also important that the meat is as lean as possible. If you feel on looking at minced meat that it looks too fatty you are better off mincing some lean meat yourself. However, as I say, it is not necessary to use the best cuts and a good quality lean braising steak is perfectly adequate.

Beef is the meat which is most commonly eaten raw, and I think it is possibly the nicest. I do like raw lamb as well, but it is rather more expensive, as only the lean parts of the meat can be used. Pork, which is the main ingredient of most air-dried and smoked meats, should not be eaten in its natural raw state, and neither should any form of poultry or game, as there is always a risk of salmonella poisoning with these.

Air-Dried and Smoked Meats

When talking about healthy foods, there is just a slight question mark over dried and smoked meats. However as people have been eating them since the Romans and even earlier – Roman soldiers used to carry their salamis in special pouches, and to lose your salami was tantamount to losing your sword – I really do not think they can be very harmful.

The reason for the question mark, is that, almost without exception, they are salted prior to smoking and they sometimes contain preservatives as well. The subject of preservatives is a very vexed one. With new EEC regulations requiring all additives to be given E numbers, naturally occurring substances, such as saltpetre, which has been used for preserving for centuries has now been given the number E252. Although doubts have been raised about saltpetre, provided meats containing it are eaten in moderation, the very small quantities present are unlikely to be harmful to the vast majority of the population, and are certainly not nearly as detrimental as eating tainted meat.

It has always been the mountainous regions which have produced the best air-dried meats and sausages, because the dry
atmosphere ensures a good, stable product. Although so many of
these meats are not factory-produced, market day in any Alpine
town or village will always find one stall packed with a plethora of
different sausages and dried meats, including beef, hams, goat, and
I regret to say, – even donkey.

Dried meats are highly nutritious: due to the weight loss that
occurs during drying the nutrients in the meat are concentrated. For
this reason, various forms of dried meat have been used all over the
world for centuries by people going on long hunting expeditions, or
to war, so that the amount they had to carry was reduced to the
minimum.

One of the hardest dried meats is biltong, which originates in
Southern Africa. The best biltong is reputed to be that made with
ostrich, but it can be made with any meat, and the strips of meat are
either sun dried or hung from the rafters of a high, draughty shed
and left until they become like leather. There is a fascinating shop
near my home where biltong made from beef, lamb, venison and
other game is produced. The proprietor is, surprisingly, not South
African in origin, but Czech, but he produces a most amazing
selection together with various smoked and dried sausages.

The North American Indians also produced a similar meat to
biltong, called jerky, with venison and buffalo, from which they
made pemmican. After drying, the meat was ground down and
mixed with an equal quantity of fat and some raw berries or cherries.
This was then formed into cakes that were packed tightly into
rawhide bags to preserve them. Early settlers copied the idea, often
using beef and raisins, and a similar mixture was made up to take on
some of the very early Arctic explorations.

In Northern Europe the pieces of meat that are dried are generally
joints, rather than strips, which means the meat in the centre is still
quite moist and, I tend to think, preferable. It is called different
names according to the country: Bundnerfleisch in Germany and
German Switzerland, Viande Sechée in France and the French
speaking part of Switzerland, and Bresaola in Italy. Beef is the meat
most commonly used, but should you find any in France or
Switzerland that appears to be slightly cheaper than usual, it is

more likely to be horse, which has a distinctive, slightly sweet flavour.

The other, most common, form of air dried meats are the raw hams of which Parma, German Westphalia and French Bayonne are the best known, although the Belgians, Dutch and Spanish all produce their own specialities. The exact method of producing the hams varies from country to country. Bayonne ham is cured in brine to which red wine is added, and is then lightly cold smoked, whereas Parma ham is dry salted for 30 to 50 days and then air-dried for three to six months. A similar meat to these hams is coppa, which is cured in exactly the same way as Parma ham, but is made from the boned pork shoulder and has a marbling of fat running through it.

When it comes to salamis and other sausages, the range is of course vast, as it encompasses not only the classic Italian, and Hungarian salamis and French saucisson sec, but German cervelat, Polish cabanos, Spanish chorizo and Hungarian guylai, as well as hundreds of other regional variations. Some of these are simply salted and air-dried, but a number of them, like guylai, are smoked as well.

Carpaccio

Named after the Venetian painter, this dish frequently appears as a starter in Italian restaurants, but the recipe does not often feature in Italian cookery books. I think this is because it is not easy to cut the meat really thinly, (it should be about as thin as Parma ham) unless you use a large piece of meat.

There are two ways round this, either buy a larger piece of meat than you need – if serving the dish as a main course for four, you will need 450 g/1 lb, but if making a starter, 350 g/12 oz will be sufficient. Cut the very thin slices off the joint and then use the remainder for another dish. Or, ask the butcher to cut you a piece of lean, good quality beef, such as topside or leg of mutton cut, and then to string it into a long, narrow round that is only about 5 cm/2 inches in diameter. From this it will be much easier to cut thin slices.

Whichever method you choose, if you pop the meat into a freezer for about ten minutes to chill it – do not actually allow it to freeze – you will find it easier to slice, and should you have a large Chinese chopper, this is even better than using a sharp knife.

METRIC/IMPERIAL	AMERICAN
350–450 g/12 oz–1 lb lean good quality beef	12 oz–1 lb lean, good quality beef
100 ml/4 fl oz French dressing (page 5) made with olive oil	½ cup French dressing (page 5) made with olive oil
1 tablespoon very finely chopped onion	1 tablespoon very finely chopped onion
1 tablespoon finely chopped capers	1 tablespoon finely chopped capers
1 tablespoon finely chopped gherkins	1 tablespoon finely chopped gherkins
1 tablespoon chopped parsley	1 tablespoon chopped parsley
4 finely chopped anchovy fillets	4 finely chopped anchovy fillets
2 teaspoons Dijon mustard	2 teaspoons Dijon mustard

Cut the meat into paper-thin slices (see above) and arrange on a serving dish. Cover with clingwrap and chill until required. Put all the remaining ingredients into a basin, whisk thoroughly together, then spoon over the centre of the meat shortly before serving.

Serves 4 (the large quantity of meat would also serve 6 as a starter)

Steak Tartare

Unquestionably the best known raw meat dish, but one for which there is not really a specific recipe, as almost everyone has their own pet variation. This is therefore a very basic version to which you can add crushed garlic, chopped chives and tarragon, finely chopped green or red chilli or peppers, grated raw beetroot, and seasonings such as Worcestershire sauce and Tabasco.

Quantities are given for one steak, as it is then easier just to adjust the ingredients according to how many you wish to serve. Also, it is one of the simplest and easiest meat dishes to prepare for one person.

METRIC/IMPERIAL	AMERICAN
100 g/4 oz lean minced beef	4 oz lean ground beef
salt and freshly milled black	salt and freshly milled black
pepper	pepper
1 egg yolk	1 egg yolk
½ small onion, finely chopped	½ small onion, finely chopped
1 tablespoon chopped parsley	1 tablespoon chopped parsley
1 tablespoon chopped capers	1 tablespoon chopped capers
2 gherkins, finely chopped	2 gherkins, finely chopped
1 rounded tablespoon mayonnaise	1 rounded tablespoon mayonnaise

Season the meat with the salt and pepper. Form into a flat cake and place in the centre of a dinner plate. Make a shallow hollow in the centre of the steak and place the egg yolk in it, if you wish this can be left in the half shell. Arrange the onion, parsley, capers, gherkins and mayonnaise in mounds round the outside of the steak. To serve, mix the seasonings into the steak with a knife and fork, using as much of the different ingredients as you require.

Serves 1

Green Peppercorn Steak

If you can get hold of them, the very best peppercorns to use for this are the fresh green ones, which are usually imported from Thailand.

Failing that, use either the kind which are preserved in brine, or dried, but if using the latter you will need slightly less.

METRIC/IMPERIAL
450 g/1 lb lean minced beef
2 teaspoons green peppercorns
1 tablespoon French mustard
salt
To serve:
about 6 button mushrooms
½ a red pepper
1 lettuce heart
4 spring onions
about 6 tablespoons thick
    mayonnaise (page 6),
    preferably made with half
    sunflower and half olive oil

AMERICAN
1 lb lean ground beef
2 teaspoons green peppercorns
1 tablespoon French mustard
salt
To serve:
about 6 button mushrooms
½ a red pepper
1 lettuce heart
4 scallions
about 6 tablespoons thick
    mayonnaise (page 6)
    preferably made with half
    sunflower and half olive oil

Put the beef into a bowl. Crush the peppercorns, ideally in a pestle and mortar, or with a knife on a board. Add to the beef with the mustard and salt and mix well. Form into four small cakes with your hands and arrange on a large serving platter.

Finely chop the button mushrooms, dice the pepper, discarding the core and seeds, shred the lettuce and chop the spring onions (scallions). Arrange them on the plate attractively in piles, together with the mayonnaise. Cover with clingwrap and chill until ready to serve.

Serves 4

Curried Beef

Plenty of freshly chopped coriander is a must for this dish, which is one of my favourite ways of eating raw beef.

METRIC/IMPERIAL	AMERICAN
450 g/1 lb lean minced beef	1 lb ground minced beef
1 small green chilli	1 small green chilli
4 tablespoons chopped coriander	4 tablespoons chopped coriander
1½ tablespoons garam masala	1½ tablespoons garam masala
2 teaspoons very finely chopped green ginger	2 teaspoons very finely chopped green ginger
5 tablespoons mayonnaise (page 6)	5 tablespoons mayonnaise (page 6)
salt and freshly milled black pepper	salt and freshly milled black pepper
To garnish:	To garnish:
1 large tomato	1 large tomato
1 lemon	1 lemon
2 tablespoons chopped coriander	2 tablespoons chopped coriander

Put the beef into a large bowl. Halve and de-seed the chilli, then chop very finely. Add to the beef with all the remaining ingredients. Beat well, then taste and adjust the seasoning. Form the meat into four round cakes and place on a serving dish. Cut the tomato and lemon into wedges. Scatter the coriander all over the beef cakes and garnish with the tomato and lemon wedges.

Serves 4

Sesame Seed Meat Balls with Tomato and Basil Mayonnaise

These very lightly spiced meat balls, with their crunchy coating of sesame seeds, team up extremely well with the tomato and basil mayonnaise on page 12. I have to be honest and admit that sesame seeds do have a slightly stronger flavour if they are toasted, so if you wish, you can cheat here and lightly toast them under a grill or in a frying pan, stirring them all the time, until they turn a golden brown.

METRIC/IMPERIAL
450 g/1 lb lean minced beef
1 tablespoon Worcestershire sauce
salt and freshly milled black
  pepper
about 3 tablespoons sesame seeds
sprigs of fresh basil
Tomato and Basil Mayonnaise
  (page 12)

AMERICAN
1 lb lean ground beef
1 tablespoon Worcestershire sauce
salt and freshly milled black
  pepper
about 3 tablespoons sesame seeds
sprigs of fresh basil
Tomato and Basil Mayonnaise
  (page 12)

Mix the beef with the Worcestershire sauce and season to taste. Form the beef into small balls, about the size of a walnut. Roll each one in the sesame seeds until it is evenly coated. Pile on to a serving dish, garnish with sprigs of fresh basil and serve with the Tomato and Basil Mayonnaise.

Serves 4

Meatballs with Horseradish Sauce

Horseradish is such a natural complement to beef, that this is an excellent way of introducing people, who might be a bit doubtful about the idea, to raw meat.

METRIC/IMPERIAL
For the meatballs:
450 g/1 lb lean minced beef
2 teaspoons freshly chopped thyme
  or ¼ teaspoon dried thyme
2 large cloves garlic, crushed
salt and freshly milled black
  pepper

AMERICAN
For the meatballs:
1 lb lean ground beef
2 teaspoons freshly chopped thyme
  or ¼ teaspoon dried thyme
2 large cloves garlic crushed
salt and freshly milled black
  pepper

For the sauce:
4 *tablespoons double cream*
3 *teaspoons grated fresh horseradish*
1 *teapoon wine vinegar*
salt and freshly milled black pepper

For the sauce:
4 *tablespoons heavy cream*
3 *teaspoons grated fresh horseradish*
1 *teaspoon wine vinegar*
salt and freshly milled black pepper

Combine the meat with the thyme, garlic and seasoning. Mix well and then form into small balls, the size of a walnut. Lightly whip the cream until it holds its shape, then fold in the horseradish and vinegar. Season to taste with salt and pepper. Pile the sauce into a small bowl and place in centre of a serving plate. Arrange the meat balls round the outside.

Serves 4

Kibbeh

The first time I ever made this was when I had to demonstrate it for a Middle Eastern video magazine, and I realized just how different it is from most European raw meat dishes, in that the meat is pounded to a complete paste. In her excellent book on *Middle Eastern Food*, Claudia Roden writes 'The pounding of the meat and wheat in a stone or metal mortar with a heavy metal pestle is a sound that wakens one in the morning and lulls one to sleep in the afternoon', which gives one a pretty good indication of just how long it takes to make by hand. Not only does it require considerable patience, but I can assure you that a strong right arm is essential as well! It can, however, be made in minutes in a food processor, which is a great blessing for those of us lucky enough to possess this modern device.

Since it is one of the staple meat dishes of the Middle East, it is not surprising that there are infinite ways of both preparing and serving it. It can be rolled into balls, or shaped into ovals, like torpedoes, or alternatively it can be served, as I have suggested here, simply pressed into a plate with lemon juice and olive oil poured over and sprinkled with chopped, preferably Continental, parsley. Lettuce, usually cos, is the traditional accompaniment, together with Arab bread, but obviously you can serve it as you wish.

METRIC/IMPERIAL	AMERICAN
100 g/4 oz burghul	2/3 cup bulgur
450 g/1 lb lean lamb	1 lb lean lamb
2 medium-sized onions	2 medium-sized onions
2 tablespoons ice-cold water	2 tablespoons ice-cold water
salt and freshly milled black pepper	salt and freshly milled black pepper
juice ½ a lemon	juice ½ a lemon
4 tablespoons olive oil	4 tablespoons olive oil
3 tablespoons chopped parsley, preferably the Continental variety	3 tablespoons chopped parsley, preferably the Continental variety

Put the burghul (bulgur) into a bowl of cold water and leave to soak for 30 minutes. Cut the meat into cubes, discarding any fat, and peel and quarter the onions. Either mince the meat finely two or three times, together with the onion, then add the seasoning and pound until the meat is very smooth, or put the meat and onion into a food processor, switch on and process until it is very smooth. Add the seasoning and the water and process or pound again.

Strain the wheat into a sieve, then squeeze out all the excess liquid with your hands. Add to the meat and either continue to pound by hand, for about 30 minutes, or process for about 3 minutes in a machine until the mixture is smooth and moist. Taste and adjust the seasoning.

Press the meat into a large dish and make a decorative pattern on the top with the blade of a knife or the handle of a spoon. Sprinkle over first the lemon juice, then the olive oil and finally scatter the parsley all over the top.

Serves 4–6

Lebanese Meatballs

Although in the Lebanon this is always made with lamb, I have made it very successfully with minced (ground) beef, which I prefer.

METRIC/IMPERIAL
450 g/1 lb lean minced lamb or
   beef
2 tablespoons tahini
4 tablespoons water
2 tablespoons olive oil
2 large cloves garlic
salt and freshly milled black
   pepper
2 tablespoons pine nuts
To garnish:
black olives
parsley

AMERICAN
1 lb lean ground lamb or beef
2 tablespoons tahini
4 tablespoons water
2 tablespoons olive oil
2 large cloves garlic
salt and freshly milled black
   pepper
2 tablespoons pine nuts
To garnish:
black olives
parsley

Turn the meat into a bowl, then beat in the tahini. Mix well, then gradually beat in the water, followed by the olive oil, beating well. Crush the garlic and add to the meat, then season to taste with salt and pepper and beat again. Stir in the pine nuts. Form into torpedo-shaped meatballs, then arrange on a serving dish and garnish with the black olives and parsley.

Serves 4

Greek Lamb

Combining some of the best Greek ingredients, this is a particularly delicately-flavoured fresh lamb dish.

METRIC/IMPERIAL	AMERICAN
450 g/1 lb lean lamb	1 lb lean lamb
2 cloves of garlic, crushed	2 cloves of garlic, crushed
4 rounded tablespoons Greek yogurt	4 rounded tablespoons Greek yogurt
1 tablespoon tahini	1 tablespoon tahini
3 tablespoons chopped coriander	3 tablespoons chopped coriander
salt and freshly milled black pepper	salt and freshly milled black pepper
To garnish:	To garnish:
2 tablespoons chopped coriander	2 tablespoons chopped coriander

Finely grind or mince the lamb, turn into a bowl and add all the remaining ingredients. Mix well and taste and adjust the seasoning, then pile into a small serving dish and sprinkle with the remaining coriander to garnish.

Serves 4

Japanese Beef

This is one recipe where it is important to use good quality beef, either fillet, sirloin or tender rump. Some supermarkets sell ready-sliced beef, that they call 'stroganoff beef' and this would be ideal.

I have given two versions of the sauce as when I tested it my guests could not decide which one they preferred, so really it all depends on whether you wish to be a purist and not use beef stock which possible gives a slightly more 'rounded' flavour. Quantities given here are for serving it as a starter, so double them if you wish to serve it as a main course.

METRIC/IMPERIAL	AMERICAN
225 g/8 oz good quality lean beef (see above)	8 oz good quality lean beef (see above)

Sauce A
1 *tablespoon soy sauce*
2 *tablespoons water*
1 *teaspoon finely chopped spring onions*
1 *teaspoon finely chopped green ginger*

Sauce B
5 *tablespoons beef stock*
scant tablespoon soy sauce
1½ *teaspoons sweet sherry*
1 *teaspoon finely chopped spring onions*
1 *teaspoon finely chopped green ginger*

Sauce A
1 *tablespoon soy sauce*
2 *tablespoons water*
1 *teaspoon finely chopped scallions*
1 *teaspoon finely chopped green ginger*

Sauce B
5 *tablespoons beef stock*
scant tablespoon soy sauce
1½ *teaspoons sweet sherry*
1 *teaspoon finely chopped scallions*
1 *teaspoon finely chopped green ginger*

Cut the meat into thin strips and arrange on four small individual plates. If you wish, you can decorate the plates with roses made from tomato skins, cut radishes etc. in the Japanese style.

For both sauces, simply mix all the ingredients together and place a quarter of it into four tiny dishes or, if you do not possess anything suitable, pour it into one dish and place it in the centre of the table.

Using chopsticks, dip each piece of meat into the sauce before eating.

Serves 4

Parma Ham with Mozarella and Figs

You want to use a really good Italian Mozerella for this; some of the Danish and other non-Italian brands are fine as a topping for pizzas, but are a poor imitation of the real thing if you want to eat it *au naturel*.

METRIC/IMPERIAL
175 g/6 oz Mozarella cheese
8 thin slices Parma ham
8 large basil leaves
To garnish:
3 ripe figs
a few basil leaves

AMERICAN
6 oz Mozarella cheese
8 thin slices Parma ham
8 large basil leaves
To garnish:
3 ripe figs
a few basil leaves

Divide the Mozarella into eight. Taking one piece of cheese at a time, loosely wrap a basil leaf round it, place on a slice of ham and roll it up. Arrange the rolls of ham on a serving platter or on four small plates.

Cut the figs into slices and use to garnish the ham, together with a few extra sprigs of basil.

Serves 4

Coppa with Cream Cheese and Peaches

You want to use one of the light French cream cheeses or fromage blanc for this recipe, as they have just the right texture and flavour to enhance both the peaches and the coppa.

METRIC/IMPERIAL
100 g/4 oz cream cheese or
  fromage blanc
12 slices of Coppa (about 100g/4
  oz)
2 ripe peaches
a squeeze of lemon juice (see
  method)

AMERICAN
½ cup cream cheese or fromage
  blanc
12 slices of Coppa, about 4 oz
2 ripe peaches
a squeeze of lemon juice (see
  method)

Divide the cheese between the slices of meat, spreading it to within about 0.75 cm/¼ inch of the edge. Peel the peaches and cut each one into six. If making this more than about an hour before serving, squeeze over a little lemon juice to preserve the colour, but this is not necessary if you are preparing and serving it straight away. Put a piece of peach on each slice of Coppa and roll up, securing each roll with a cocktail stick if necessary.

Serves 4

Bresaola with Pears

I came upon this combination quite by chance having experimented with soaking some dried pears in red wine and then wondering what to do with them. However, it is a superb combination and well worth the minor effort of soaking the pears in the wine overnight.

METRIC/IMPERIAL
6 dried pear halves
100 ml/4 fl oz red wine
12 slices bresaola (about 175 g/6 oz)
6 tablespoons mayonnaise (page 6)

AMERICAN
6 dried pear halves
1 cup red wine
12 slices bresaola (about 6 oz)
6 tablespoons mayonnaise (page 6)

Soak the pear halves overnight or for up to 36 hours in the wine, turning them from time to time, then remove from the wine and cut each one in half lengthways. Spread each slice of bresaola with some of the mayonnaise and place a pear quarter in each one. Roll up and secure with cocktail sticks, if necessary, and arrange on a serving platter.

Serves 4 as a starter

Pineapple and Celery Salad with Smoked Sausage

You can use any of the spiced, smoked sausages for this, like Cabanos, guylai or chorizo. The pineapple can also be interchanged with chopped dessert apple if this is more readily available.

METRIC/IMPERIAL
1 *head of celery*
½ *medium-sized pineapple*
175 *g/6 oz smoked sausage*
50 *g/2 oz walnuts*
200 *ml/8 fl oz mayonnaise (page 6)*
salt and freshly milled black pepper

AMERICAN
1 *head of celery*
½ *medium-sized pineapple*
6 *oz smoked sausage*
½ *cup walnuts*
1 *cup mayonnaise (page 6)*
salt and freshly milled black pepper

Discard any very coarse outer leaves of the celery and finely chop the remainder, reserving the leaves for garnishing. Peel the pineapple, remove the core and all the eyes and chop finely. Remove any tough outer skin, if possible, from the smoked sausage and chop into pieces about 0.75 cm/¼ inch thick. Coarsely chop the walnuts. Put all the ingredients into a large bowl. Mix well and season to taste with salt and pepper. Pile into a serving dish and garnish with the reserved celery leaves.

Serves 6 as a starter, 4 as a main course

Salami with Fennel in French Dressing

The best kind of sausage to use for this is one of the chunky, whole ones which you can buy in a number of delicatessens and supermarkets.

METRIC/IMPERIAL	AMERICAN
225 g/8 oz salami or similar sausage	8 oz salami or similar sausage
2 fennel bulbs	2 heads of fennel
4 tablespoons olive oil	4 tablespoons olive oil
1 teaspoon coriander seeds	1 teaspoon coriander seeds
1 tablespoon finely chopped onion	1 tablespoon finely chopped onion
2 teaspoons finely chopped capers	2 teaspoons finely chopped capers
2 tablespoons chopped parsley	2 tablespoons chopped parsley
freshly milled black pepper	freshly milled black pepper

Cut the salami or sausage into slices about an eighth inch/0.5 cm thick. Arrange them in a shallow dish. Finely chop the fennel, discarding any tough outer stalks and scatter over the salami. Roughly crush the coriander seeds and mix them with the oil, onion, capers, parsley and pepper. Spoon over the salami and fennel, cover with clingwrap and put into the fridge or a cool place to marinate for eight hours before serving.

Serves 4

Moravian Salad

You want to make this Czechoslovakian salad with a spiced smoked Polish or Hungarian sausage, like cabanos or guylai, if possible. Failing that choose a Spanish chorizo or a highly spiced salami.

METRIC/IMPERIAL	AMERICAN
225 g/ 8 oz smoked sausage	8 oz smoked sausage
2 dill cucumbers	2 dill pickles
100 g/4 oz white cabbage	4 oz white cabbage
1 dessert apple	1 dessert apple
1 tablespoon lemon juice	1 tablespoon lemon juice
1 tablespoon fresh or 1 teaspoon dried dill	1 tablespoon fresh or 1 teaspoon dried dill

150 ml/¼ pint soured cream	⅝ cup sour cream
a little top of the milk, if necessary	a little top of the milk, if necessary
salt and freshly milled black pepper	salt and freshly milled black pepper

Cut the smoked sausage into thin strips or dice. Put into a bowl. Finely chop the cucumbers (pickle), finely shred the cabbage, and add to the meat. Core and dice the apple, then toss in lemon juice to preserve the colour. Add to the meat with the dill. Fold the cream into the salad, adding a little top of the milk, if the mixture is too stiff. Season to taste with salt and pepper. Chill for at least one hour before serving to allow the flavours to infuse.

Serves 4

Cervelat Salad

Mild-flavoured German cervelat makes a good, fairly inexpensive salad, as it is considerably cheaper than the Italian and French salamis.

METRIC/IMPERIAL
225 g/8 oz cervelat, cut in one
    piece
100 g/4 oz mushrooms
¼ cucumber
1 small bunch radishes
4 spring onions
2 tablespoons chopped parsley
6 tablespoons French dressing
    made with sunflower oil (page
    5)
2 tablespoons sunflower seeds

AMERICAN
8 oz cervelat, cut in one piece
4 oz mushrooms
¼ cucumber
1 small bunch radishes
4 scallions
2 tablespoons chopped parsley
6 tablespoons French dressing
    made with sunflower oil (page
    5)
2 tablespoons sunflower seeds

Peel off the skin of the cervelat and dice. Slice the mushrooms, dice the cucumber, slice the radishes and chop the onions (scallions).

Put all the ingredients into a serving bowl with the parsley. Pour over the French dressing, toss lightly together and leave for at least 30 minutes for the flavours to infuse before serving, sprinkled with the sunflower seeds.

Serves 4

CHEESE

If folklore is to be believed, cheese originated with a nomadic tribe in the Middle East. According to legend, the tribe had tried making cheese, simply by allowing the milk to sour naturally, but the result was acid-tasting and not very palatable. One day a herdsman put some milk into an improperly-cured pouch he had made from the lining of a young goat's stomach. The result was a sweet-tasting curd, because the rennet that still remained in the lining of the stomach curdled the milk, separating it into curds and whey.

It is with this basic process that all cheese, except some of the fresh curd and cream cheeses, commences. For this reason, both vegetarian and kosher cheeses are made as strict vegetarians, and strict Jews will not eat cheese that has been started with rennet, but instead only eat cheeses that have been curdled by the action of plant extracts.

I never cease to be amazed by just how many different cheeses there are, with such completely varying flavours. The fact that such diverse cheeses as Brie, Cheddar and Gorgonzola are all made with cow's milk only goes to prove what an art cheese-making is. Cow's milk is by far the milk most commonly used, but the milk of any animal can be made into cheese. Goat's milk is being used more frequently as the soft 'chèvres' of France become increasingly popular, as is Greek feta (although this is frequently made with cow's milk). A true Mozzarella should be made with buffalo's milk, whilst that king of the French blue-veined cheeses, Roquefort, is made with ewe's milk.

Most cheeses are technically 'raw'. The curds, for example, of Brie and Camembert are never heated, but those that are used for the hard cheeses such as Cheddar and Leicester are scalded to a temperature of 40°C/110°F and then pressed, and those of Gruyère and Emmenthal are subjected to 60°C/150°F before being pressed. The amount of time a cheese is pressed for, or is left to ripen, depends on the type; a Brie or Camembert, which is not pressed so that the whey drains away naturally, will be ready for eating in about a month. A Cheshire, which is lightly pressed, will have matured in about six weeks, whilst a strong Cheddar can take from nine to twelve months.

Cheese is highly nutritious, as it is effectively concentrated milk. Cheddar, the most popular cheese in both the UK and the US, contains 40% water, 29% fat, 25% protein, 4% vitamins and minerals (it is a good source of Vitamins A, D, E, riboflavin, and phospherous and calcium) and 2% carbohydrate. It contains no fibre.

These constituents will, of course, vary with different cheeses, the most significant difference being in the fat content depending on whether the cheese has been made with whole or skimmed milk. Almost all cheeses state on them what their fat content is, so if you are concerned about your cholestrol intake, it is not difficult to choose cheeses which have a lower level of fat. However, when talking about cholestrol, it should be borne in mind that *some* cholestrol is essential for the healthy functioning of the body.

Whilst it is not practical to attempt to make most cheeses at home, it is not difficult to make your own fresh curd cheese, or even a yogurt cheese. These are not true cheeses in that the yogurt is not soured or curdled, but both are excellent on their own; with bread or vegetables; mixed with chopped fresh herbs; or with sugar (or honey) and fruit to make a simple dessert.

To Make Curd Cheese

There are two ways of making this.
1. Allow about 3 pints/1.8 litres of whole or skimmed milk to sour. Do this as quickly as possible so that no mould forms on the curds. Line a large sieve or colander with a piece of muslin, pour in the milk, then bring the corners together and tie with a piece of string. Hang up the muslin bag and leave to drain for 12 to 24 hours.
2. To make the cheese more quickly, bring the same quantity of fresh milk just up to blood heat in a saucepan. Add 4 teaspoons of rennet and leave in a warm place or until the milk has set. Stir well, then spoon this into the muslin and leave to drain, as above, for 12 to 24 hours.

To Make Yogurt Cheese

Line a colander with muslin, as above. Pour in 600 ml/1 pint natural yogurt, then hang up the bag and leave to drain for 12 hours.

Liptauer Cheese Spread

There are endless variations of this cheese spread, which is made throughout Germany, Austria and Hungary, but in this recipe, I have deliberately increased the quantity of ale to make a very light spread, which is perfect with crackers, or can just as easily be used as a dip with crudités.

METRIC/IMPERIAL	AMERICAN
225 g/8 oz cream cheese	1 cup cream cheese
50 g/2 oz softened butter	¼ cup softened butter
½ teaspoon dry mustard	½ teaspoon dry mustard
1 tablespoon paprika	1 tablespoon paprika
2 tablespoons soured cream	2 tablespoons sour cream
2 teaspoons chopped capers	2 teaspoons chopped capers
4 tablespoons light ale or beer	4 tablespoons light ale or beer
salt	salt

Beat the cheese, then beat in the butter, mustard and paprika. Beat in all the remaining ingredients and season to taste with salt. Turn into a serving dish and chill until ready to serve.

Blue Cheese Roll

With its bright green coating of parsley, this roll can give a striking contrast and add interest to a very basic cheeseboard.

METRIC/IMPERIAL	AMERICAN
225 g/8 oz double cream cheese	8 oz double cream cheese
50 g/2 oz Danish Blue cheese	2 oz Danish Blue cheese
4 tablespoons chopped parsley	4 tablespoons chopped parsley

Lightly beat the cream cheese. Crumble in the Danish Blue, then beat well together. Sprinkle the parsley over a piece of greaseproof or non-stick paper. Form the cheese into a roll about 15 cm/6 inches long and roll in the parsley.

Roll up in the paper, place on a plate and refrigerate for at least 1 hour before serving.

Serves 4

Potted Cheese

In the days of 'waste not, want not', people really knew how to use up every last scrap of food, and turn it into something special. This old English recipe is a typical example. It is undoubtedly one of the very best ways of using up a piece of cheese that has seen a day or so too many on the cheeseboard. You can use any of the hard cheeses for this from Cheshire, Double Gloucester and Cheddar, to Wensleydale and Lancashire.

METRIC/IMPERIAL
225 g/8 oz hard cheese (see above)
75 g/3 oz butter, preferably
    unsalted
2 tablespoons port or brown sherry
1 tablespoon chopped chives or 1
    teaspoon caraway seeds
pinch cayenne pepper
To garnish:
a few walnut halves

AMERICAN
8 oz hard cheese (see above)
3/8 cup butter, preferably sweet
2 tablespoons port or brown sherry
1 tablespoon chopped chives or 1
    teaspoon caraway seeds
pinch cayenne pepper
To garnish:
a few walnut halves

Finely grate the cheese. Cream the butter, then gradually beat in the grated cheese. Stir in the port or sherry, chives or caraway seeds and cayenne and blend well. Spoon into a pot, smooth over the top and chill for at least one hour. Garnish with the walnut halves before serving.

Serves 4–6

Cottage Cheese with Spinach

I have never been a fan of cottage cheese 'au naturel', finding it rather bland and tasteless, but it is good as a vehicle for adding other flavours. This very simple mixture would make a good light lunch, especially for anyone who is slimming, in which case you should omit the mayonnaise which just adds a little extra flavour.

METRIC/IMPERIAL
about 8 young spinach leaves
3 spring onions
225 g/8 oz cottage cheese
2 tablespoons mayonnaise (page
    6)
salt and freshly milled black
    pepper

AMERICAN
about 8 young spinach leaves
3 scallions
1 cup cottage cheese
2 tablespoons mayonnaise (page
    6)
salt and freshly milled black
    pepper

Wash and dry the spinach leaves and shred them finely, discarding the stalks. Finely chop the spring onions (scallions), put them into a basin with the cottage cheese and mayonnaise and mix well, then season to taste with salt and pepper.

Serves 2

Stuffed Dates

Fresh dates bear little resemblance to the incredibly sweet and sticky dried ones which were considered a Christmas treat when I was a child. They are now imported throughout the year, mainly from Israel, and can be used in both sweet and savoury salads. They are also excellent stuffed and while they can be filled with mixtures such as marzipan, chocolate butter cream, shelled nuts, or other fruits such as segments of tangerine, they are quite delicious stuffed with cheese. Although you can use any cheese you like provided it has some 'bite' to it, such as a sharp Cheddar or Caerphilly, I think undoubtedly one of the most superb combinations is fresh dates with feta cheese – once tried, never forgotten!

Celery and Tomato Cheesecake

A really good vegetarian main course, which is perfect served with chunky granary bread and a tossed green salad.

METRIC/IMPERIAL	AMERICAN
50 g/2 oz walnuts	½ cup walnuts
75 g/3 oz Cheddar cheese	3 oz Cheddar cheese
For the filling:	For the filling:
450 g/1 lb curd cheese	2 cups curd cheese

300 ml/½ pint half cream	1¼ cups half cream
2 sticks celery	2 sticks celery
2 cloves garlic	2 cloves garlic
4 tablespoons chopped parsley	4 tablespoons chopped parsley
salt and freshly milled black pepper	salt and freshly milled black pepper
15 g/½ oz or 1 envelope powdered gelatine	1 envelope unflavoured gelatin
450 g/1 lb tomatoes	1 lb tomatoes

Coarsely grind the walnuts and finely grate the cheese. Blend them together, then press into the base of a 17.5 cm/7 inch loose-bottomed cake tin or spring form pan. Put into the refrigerator to chill while preparing the filling.

Beat the curd cheese, then beat in the cream. Finely chop the celery and crush the garlic and add to the cheese together with the parsley. Beat well together, and season to taste with salt and pepper.

Sprinkle the gelatine (gelatin) over the water in a small cup or basin and leave to soften for five minutes. Stand over a pan of hot water and leave until the gelatine has completely dissolved, then stir into the cheese mixture and beat well.

Spoon half the mixture into the tin and place in the refrigerator for about 45 minutes or until it is set. Slice half the tomatoes and arrange on the top. Season with salt and pepper and spoon over the remainder of the cheesecake mixture. Chill for at least two hours or until set.

Remove from the refrigerator and take out of the tin. Slip a spatula under the base and carefully slide the cheesecake on to a serving dish. Slice the remainder of the tomatoes and use to decorate the top of the cheesecake.

Serves 6–8

Salami and Avocado Cheesecake

The base for this cheesecake is made with ground raw cashew nuts and tahina which contrasts well with the avocado mixture.

METRIC/IMPERIAL

For the base:

100 g/4 oz cashew nuts

1 tablespoon tahina

For the cheesecake:

2 ripe avocados

225 g/8 oz curd cheese

¼ pint single cream

juice ½ a lemon

5 rounded tablespoons mayonnaise
  (page 6)

15 g/½ oz or 1 envelope powdered
  gelatine

4 tablespoons water

75 g/3 oz salami

salt and freshly milled black
  pepper

To garnish:

25 g/1 oz salami

AMERICAN

For the base:

1 cup shelled cashew nuts

1 tablespoon tahina

For the cheesecake:

2 ripe avocados

1 cup curd cheese

⅝ cup light cream

juice ½ a lemon

5 rounded tablespoons mayonnaise
  (page 6)

1 envelope unflavored gelatin

4 tablespoons water

3 oz salami

salt and freshly milled black
  pepper

To garnish:

1 oz salami

Grind the cashew nuts in a blender or food processor until they are fairly smooth. Add the tahina and whizz quickly again. Press the mixture into the base of a lightly oiled 17.5 cm/7 inch springform pan or loose-bottomed cake tin. Chill while preparing the mixture.

Halve the avocados, remove the stones and scoop out the flesh. Purée the avocado in a blender or food processor, then add the cheese, cream, lemon juice and mayonnaise and whizz again. Sprinkle the gelatine (gelatin) over the water in a basin and leave to soften for five minutes. Stand the basin over a pan of gently simmering water until the gelatine has completely dissolved. Add to the avocado mixture. Cut the salami into thin matchsticks and add to the avocado mixture and season to taste with salt and freshly milled black pepper. Turn into the prepared tin and leave for at least three hours until set.

To remove from the tin, loosen the edges of the cheesecake with a knife, then push up the bottom of the tin, or simply release if using a springform pan. Slide the cheesecake on to a serving dish. To garnish the cheesecake, make a cut into the slices of salami to the centre, then twist the slices round to form a cornet. Arrange these on the top of the cheesecake.

Serves 4–6 as a main course, or 8 as a starter

Gorgonzola Mousse

This mousse is wonderful served with a simple tossed green salad, and a few sliced tomatoes flavoured with a little chopped basil.

METRIC/IMPERIAL	AMERICAN
225 g/8 oz Gorgonzola	8 oz Gorgonzola
225 g/8 oz curd cheese	1 cup curd cheese
2 eggs, separated	2 eggs, separated
150 ml/¼ pint soured cream	⅝ cup sour cream
2 teaspoons powdered gelatine	2 teaspoons unflavored gelatin
2 tablespoons water	2 tablespoons water
salt and freshly milled black pepper	salt and freshly milled black pepper
To garnish:	To garnish:
1 tomato	1 tomato
a few celery leaves	a few celery leaves

Mash the Gorgonzola, removing all the rind. Add the curd cheese and egg yolks and beat well, then beat in the cream. Sprinkle the gelatine (gelatin) over the water in a cup or small basin and leave to soften for five minutes. Stand over a pan of hot water until the gelatine is completely dissolved, then beat into the cheese mixture. Season to taste with salt and plenty of freshly milled black pepper. Whisk the egg whites until they form stiff peaks and fold into the mixture. Turn into a serving dish and chill for at least one hour. Quarter the tomato and garnish the mousse with the celery and tomato before serving.

Serves 6 as a starter, 4 as a main course

Mange Tout (Snow Peas) with Feta Cheese and Basil

Crisp mange tout or snow peas make an interesting salad, and they are also excellent served as crudités with dips.

METRIC/IMPERIAL	AMERICAN
225 g/8 oz mange tout	8 oz snow peas
3 sprigs of basil	3 sprigs of basil
100 g/4 oz feta cheese	4 oz feta cheese
2 tablespoons olive oil (ideally use a virgin oil for this)	2 tablespoons olive oil (ideally use a virgin oil for this)
freshly milled black pepper	freshly milled black pepper

String the mange tout (snow peas) and arrange in a serving dish. Coarsely chop the basil, crumble the feta and scatter them over the mange tout. Pour over the olive oil and season well with plenty of freshly milled black pepper.

Serves 4

Baby Corn with Blue Brie

Little baby corn have a wonderful delicate flavour as well as a good crunchy texture, which makes them a welcome addition to a number of salads.

METRIC/IMPERIAL	AMERICAN
225 g/8 oz baby corn	8 oz baby corn
½ a cucumber	½ a cucumber
salt and freshly milled black pepper	salt and freshly milled black pepper
100 g/4 oz blue Brie	4 oz blue Brie
5 tablespoons French dressing made with sunflower or grape seed oil (page 5)	5 tablespoons French dressing made with sunflower or grape seed oil (page 5)

Unless they are very small, cut the corn in half lengthways, and then across into half again. Cut the cucumber into 1.25 cm/¼ inch dice. Season with salt and pepper. Break the cheese into 0.75 cm/¼ inch pieces and add to the corn. Pour over the French dressing just before serving and toss lightly.

Serves 4

Spinach, Mushroom and Feta Salad

Although you can use a dressing made with olive or sunflower oil for this salad, it is really quite superb if tossed in one made with walnut or hazelnut oil.

METRIC/IMPERIAL
225 g/8 oz young spinach leaves
225 g/8 oz button mushrooms
100 g/4 oz feta cheese
6 tablespoons French dressing
  (page 5)

AMERICAN
8 oz young spinach leaves
8 oz button mushrooms
4 oz feta cheese
6 tablespoons French dressing
  (page 5)

Discard the stalks from the spinach, wash well and dry thoroughly. Tear the larger leaves into slightly smaller pieces and quarter the mushrooms. Turn into a salad bowl and crumble over the cheese. Pour over the dressing and toss lightly before serving.

Serves 4–6

Carrot and Sage Derby Salad

Sage Derby is a rather under-rated English cheese, whose flavour combines well with a number of vegetables.

METRIC/IMPERIAL	AMERICAN
450 g/1 lb carrots	1 lb carrots
175 g/6 oz sage Derby	6 oz sage Derby
100 g/4 oz mushrooms	4 oz mushrooms
4 tablespoons French dressing made with sunflower or olive oil (page 5)	4 tablespoons French dressing made with sunflower or olive oil (page 5)

Peel the carrots and grate them. Grate the cheese and slice the mushrooms thinly. Put into a large bowl, add the French dressing and toss lightly together.

Serves 4

Danish Blue Cauliflower

Perfect for a light lunch served with thinly sliced raw ham or mild salami

METRIC/IMPERIAL	AMERICAN
150 ml/¼ pint natural yogurt	⅝ cup natural yogurt
50 g/2 oz Danish Blue cheese	2 oz Danish Blue cheese
salt and freshly milled black pepper	salt and freshly milled black pepper
225 g/8 oz cauliflower florets	8 oz cauliflower florets
To garnish:	To garnish:
4 medium-sized tomatoes	4 medium-sized tomatoes

Mix the yogurt with the blue cheese and season to taste with a little salt and plenty of freshly milled black pepper. Break the cauliflower into florets. Toss in the dressing and leave for about 30 minutes for the flavours to infuse. Pile into the centre of a serving dish. Slice the tomatoes, arrange them round the edge of the dish and season them with salt and pepper.

Serves 3–4

Green Salad with Anchovies and Parmesan Cheese

You really want a good mixture of lettuces and other salad stuff for this; some crisp Webbs or Iceburg lettuce, perhaps a little Cos and some watercress, mustard and cress and chicory and/or endive as well. Parmesan cheese keeps for months and months in the fridge, so it is well worth buying a whole piece and grating it when you need it as the flavour is greatly superior to that bought ready-grated.

METRIC/IMPERIAL
350 g/12 oz green salad stuff (see above)
40 g/1¾ oz can anchovies
4 tablespoons olive oil
2 tablespoons red wine vinegar
salt and freshly milled black pepper
2 tablespoons grated Parmesan cheese

AMERICAN
12 oz green salad stuff (see above)
1¾ oz can anchovies
4 tablespoons olive oil
2 tablespoons red wine vinegar
salt and freshly milled black pepper
2 tablespoons grated Parmesan cheese

Wash and thoroughly dry all the salad. Place in a salad bowl, cover with clingwrap and chill until ready to serve.

Drain the oil from the anchovies and mix with the olive oil, vinegar and seasoning. Add the cheese and whisk lightly together. Finely chop the anchovies and add to the dressing. Just before serving, whisk the dressing once more, pour over the salad and toss lightly together.

Serves 4

Winter Salad with Goat's Cheese

Winter salads have now been transformed by the availability of curly

91

endive, lambs' tongues lettuce (also known as mâche) and the vivid red Italian radicchio.

METRIC/IMPERIAL	AMERICAN
225 g/8 oz curly endive	8 oz curly endive
100 g/4 oz lambs' tongues lettuce	4 oz lambs' tongues lettuce
100 g/4 oz radicchio	4 oz radicchio
salt and freshly milled black pepper	salt and freshly milled black pepper
175 g/6 oz goat's cheese	6 oz goat's cheese
75 g/3 oz walnuts	¾ cup walnuts
6 tablespoons French dressing (page 5) made with half olive and half sunflower oil	6 tablespoons French dressing (page 5) made with half olive and half sunflower oil

Wash and thoroughly dry the endive, lambs' tongues lettuce and radicchio. Roughly tear the pieces and put into a large salad bowl. Season with a little salt and plenty of freshly milled black pepper. Remove the rind from the goat's cheese and crumble the remainder. Coarsely chop the walnuts. Scatter the goat's cheese and walnuts over the salad. Pour over the dressing just before serving and toss lightly.

Serves 4

Roquefort Pear Salad

Not a new recipe, but the combination of blue cheese and pears never fails to be popular. Although Roquefort does give you the best flavour, it is easily one of the most expensive cheeses, so it could be replaced with Danish Blue or Dolcelatte.

METRIC/IMPERIAL	AMERICAN
4 ripe dessert pears	4 ripe dessert pears
lemon juice (see below)	lemon juice (see below)

50 g/2 oz Roquefort cheese	2 oz Roquefort cheese
50 g/2 oz cream cheese	¼ cup cream cheese
2 tablespoons mayonnaise (page 6)	2 tablespoons mayonnaise (page 6)
1 tablespoon chopped walnuts	1 tablespoon chopped walnuts
a little single or half cream (see below)	a little light or half cream (see below)
salt and freshly milled black pepper	salt and freshly milled black pepper
To garnish:	To garnish:
lettuce leaves	lettuce leaves
paprika	paprika

Peel and halve the pears, scoop out the cores with a spoon and dip the fruit quickly in lemon juice to preserve its colour. Place on a serving dish. Mash the Roquefort with the cream cheese and mayonnaise. Add the walnuts, then soften the dressing with sufficient cream to give a good coating consistency. Season to taste with salt and pepper and spoon the dressing over the pears. Garnish with a few crisp lettuce leaves and sprinkle with paprika just before serving.

Serves 4

Stuffed Peaches with Cheese

Ideally you want to use the large, yellow-fleshed peaches for this starter, in which the cavity where the stone has been removed is stuffed with a mixture of Cheddar and Parmesan cheese, and then a creamy cheese dressing is poured over the top. If you prefer, large nectarines could be used instead, in which case it is not necessary to peel them.

METRIC/IMPERIAL	AMERICAN
3 large peaches	3 large peaches

1 tablespoon lemon juice or
  tarragon vinegar
75 g/3 oz Cheddar cheese
25 g/1 oz butter
2 tablespoons grated Parmesan
  cheese
pinch of cayenne pepper
75 g/3 oz cream cheese
150 ml/¼ pint single cream
salt and freshly milled black
  pepper
To garnish:
paprika
mustard and cress

1 tablespoon lemon juice or
  tarragon vinegar
3 oz Cheddar cheese
2 tablespoons butter
2 tablespoons grated Parmesan
  cheese
pinch of cayenne pepper
3/8 cup cream cheese
⅝ cup light cream
salt and freshly milled black
  pepper
To garnish:
paprika
mustard and cress

Peel the peaches, halve and stone them. If they are difficult to peel, dip them very quickly in boiling water. Brush each peach half all over with a very little tarragon vinegar or lemon juice to preserve the colour.

Finely grate the Cheddar cheese. Cream the butter, beat in the Cheddar and Parmesan and season with cayenne pepper. Form into six balls and use to fill the cavities in the peaches where the stones were removed.

Place a stuffed peach, cut side down on six small plates. Beat the cream cheese and gradually beat in the cream to give a good coating consistency. Season to taste with salt and pepper. Pour over the peach halves, sprinkle with a little paprika and garnish each one with a small bunch of cress.

Serves 6

Raspberry Salad with Blue Cheese Dressing

This may seem a rather bizarre combination, but it works surprisingly well. You need to use fresh raspberries, as frozen raspberries have too much liquid in them.

CHEESE

METRIC/IMPERIAL	AMERICAN
50 g/2 oz Danish Blue cheese	2 oz Danish Blue cheese
4 tablespoons mayonnaise (page 6)	4 tablespoons mayonnaise (page 6)
225 g/8 oz fresh raspberries	8 oz fresh raspberries
salt and freshly milled black pepper	salt and freshly milled black pepper
¼ cucumber	¼ cucumber

Finely crumble the cheese, and stir into the mayonnaise, blend well. Carefully fold in the raspberries taking care not to break them. Season with a little salt, if necessary, and some pepper. Thinly slice the cucumber and arrange round the edge of a serving plate and pile the raspberry mixture into the centre.

Serves 3–4

VEGETABLES AND SALADS

It is well known that you obtain the maximum amount of nutrients from both vegetables and fruit by eating them raw. Not only are many of the minerals and vitamins destroyed by heat, but the cell structure is changed, making them harder to digest for many people.

The biggest problem with eating vegetables raw is monotony, and certainly if all one ever ate were crudités, no matter how exquisitely they were prepared, the boredom level would be very high. What makes salads interesting is the different combinations one can try and, more importantly, the different dressings.

Even a simple green salad can be endlessly varied, not only by using a different combination of lettuces, instead of just one, but by the addition of herbs such as parsley, basil, chives, mint, chervil, and chopped fennel. Just using a different oil or vinegar to make a basic French dressing can also completely change the flavour of the entire dish.

The seasons of the year play an important part in our body's metabolism. In the summer one wants light, delicate salads, using the ingredients which have traditionally been available, while in the winter rather more robust numbers made with endive, crisp cabbage, Brussels sprouts and root vegetables feel more appropriate.

But this is not the only role that seasons play. Although it is quite possible to grow tomatoes, peppers, aubergines (egg plants), and cucumbers in greenhouses throughout the year, so often, while very appealing to the eye, these vegetables are completely tasteless. They need sunshine – the genuine article – to ripen them and give them flavour, and if deprived of it they will never have the same heady scent and flavour.

Freshness is just as vital for vegetables as it is for meat and fish, albeit for a different reason. Meat and fish must be fresh to reduce any risk of bacteria, but vegetables, particularly the green ones, lose a number of valuable nutrients once they have been picked. Thus, a fresh lettuce or cabbage will not only look and taste better than a tired one, but it will also be better for you and your digestive system. Similarly, if vegetables are to be served grated or shredded, it is best not to prepare them too long before serving, as small amounts of nutrients in them will be lost.

The range of vegetables one can eat raw is not restricted to what I would describe as the 'classic' salad ingredients. Salads can be made with almost any vegetable you can think of, including French and runner beans, peas and mange tout (snow peas), young turnip, beetroot, broccoli, courgettes (zucchini) and marrows.

Nor, in fact, do you have to make them all into salads. I used to drive my father, a keen gardener, mad by going down the garden and eating all his beans and peas straight off the vine. If you have that opportunity, it is not one to pass up – there really are few better meals to be had!

Guacamole Stuffed Tomatoes

To be honest, this filling is not a true guacamole but more a piquant avocado purée. However it looks very pretty and tastes sublime, provided it is made with well-flavoured tomatoes.

METRIC/IMPERIAL	AMERICAN
4 small beefsteak tomatoes	4 small beefsteak tomatoes
salt and freshly milled black pepper	salt and freshly milled black pepper
2 cloves garlic	2 cloves garlic
2 small ripe avocados	2 small ripe avocados
5 tablespoons mayonnaise (page 6)	5 tablespoons mayonnaise (page 6)
a good dash Tabasco	a good dash Tabasco
2.5 cm/1 inch piece cucumber	1 inch piece cucumber
To garnish:	To garnish:
paprika	paprika

Cut the tops off the tomatoes and scoop out the insides with a teaspoon. Season the insides with salt and pepper. Crush the garlic. Halve the avocados, remove the stones and peel. Mash the pulp and beat in the mayonnaise and garlic. Season to taste with salt, black pepper and Tabasco. Chop the tomato lids and cucumber into 0.75 cm/¼ inch dice and add to the avocado mixture. Pile into the tomato cases and arrange on individual serving dishes. Sprinkle with a little paprika before serving.

Serves 4

Stuffed Cherry Tomatoes

Although slightly fiddly to prepare, these tomatoes look very pretty and make a delicious nibble to serve with drinks.

METRIC/IMPERIAL	AMERICAN
450 g/1 lb cherry tomatoes	1 lb cherry tomatoes
225 g/8 oz curd cheese	1 cup curd cheese
2–3 sprigs of basil	2–3 sprigs of basil
salt and freshly milled black pepper	salt and freshly milled black pepper

Slice the tops off the tomatoes, and scoop out seeds with a small teaspoon. Beat the curd cheese. Chop the basil discarding any coarse stalks and add to curd cheese. Season to taste with salt and pepper. Using two teaspoons, put a good teaspoonful of the mixture into each of the tomatoes.

Makes approx. 28

Avocados with Strawberry Sauce

An unusual combination, but the flavours mingle well and it looks startlingly pretty with the greens of the avocado and lime and the pink of the strawberries.

METRIC/IMPERIAL	AMERICAN
2 large ripe avocados	2 large ripe avocados
juice 1 lime	juice 1 lime
3 tablespoons sunflower oil	3 tablespoons sunflower oil
100 g/4 oz strawberries	4 oz strawberries
about 2 teaspoons sugar	about 2 teaspoons sugar
salt and freshly milled black pepper	salt and freshly milled black pepper
To garnish:	To garnish:
1 lime	1 lime

Halve the avocados, take out the stones and peel them. Cut into slices, then divide them between four small plates, arranging them attractively. Brush all over with half the lime juice, to preserve the colour.

Put the oil, remaining lime juice, strawberries and sugar into a blender or food processor and whizz until smooth. Taste, add a little more sugar if necessary, then season with salt and pepper. Spoon the sauce on to the avocado slices, but leaving about half of each slice still exposed.

Cut the lime for garnish into slices and use to decorate each plate.

Serves 4

Avocado and Watercress Mousse with Lumpfish Roe

This mousse really does taste as good as it looks, the black of the lumpfish roe contrasting well with the pale green mousse.

METRIC/IMPERIAL
1 large ripe avocado
1 medium-sized bunch watercress
150 ml/¼ pint soured cream
6 tablespoons mayonnaise (page 6)
juice ½ a lemon
2 tablespoons water
15 g/½ oz or 1 envelope powdered gelatine
salt and freshly milled black pepper
2 egg whites
To garnish:
50 g/2 oz lumpfish roe
a few sprigs watercress

AMERICAN
1 large ripe avocado
1 medium-sized bunch watercress
⅝ cup sour cream
6 tablespoons mayonnaise (page 6)
juice ½ a lemon
2 tablespoons water
1 envelope unflavored gelatin
salt and freshly milled black pepper
2 egg whites
To garnish:
2 oz lumpfish roe
a few sprigs watercress

Halve the avocado, remove the stone, peel and either mash the flesh or purée in a blender or food processor. Very finely chop the watercress and add to the avocado in a bowl, together with three-quarters of the cream, and the mayonnaise.

Pour the lemon juice and water into a small cup or bowl, sprinkle over the gelatine (gelatin) and leave to stand for five minutes, then stand over a pan of gently simmering water and leave until the gelatine has completely dissolved. Remove from the heat and beat into the avocado mixture. Season well with salt and freshly milled black pepper; you are likely to need a good deal more seasoning than you expect, especially black pepper.

Whisk the egg whites until they are stiff, then fold into the mixture. Turn into a lightly oiled 15 cm/6 inch cake tin and chill in the refrigerator for at least two hours or until set.

To turn out the mousse, dip the tin into a bowl of very hot water, then invert on to a serving dish and remove the tin. Spread the remaining soured (sour) cream over the centre of the mousse, then pile the lumpfish roe on top. Garnish round the edge of the mousse with the sprigs of watercress.

Serves 6 as a starter or 4 as a main course

Walnut and Avocado Salad

Although this salad can be served as a starter, served with another salad it will also make a light lunch or supper as the mixture of avocado and nuts makes it very high in protein.

METRIC/IMPERIAL	AMERICAN
2 avocados	2 avocados
2 tablespoons lemon juice	2 tablespoons lemon juice
2 cloves garlic	2 cloves garlic
50 g/2 oz walnuts	½ cup walnuts
2 dessert apples	2 dessert apples
3 tablespoons olive oil	3 tablespoons olive oil
good pinch dry mustard	good pinch dry mustard
salt and freshly milled black pepper	salt and freshly milled black pepper
To garnish:	To garnish:
2 tomatoes	2 tomatoes
about 12 black olives	about 12 black olives

Cut the avocados in half, remove the stones and carefully scoop out the flesh, taking care not to spoil the skin. Mash the flesh with the lemon juice. Crush the garlic and finely chop the walnuts. Peel and core the apples and chop finely. Add to the avocado purée with the walnuts, garlic, olive oil and mustard. Mix well and season to taste with salt and freshly milled black pepper. Pile the mixture back into the avocado shells and arrange on individual plates. Slice the tomatoes, stone the olives and chop them coarsely. Use them to garnish the avocados.

Serves 4

Watercress Fool

An elegant starter for a dinner party.

METRIC/IMPERIAL	AMERICAN
1 large bunch watercress	1 large bunch watercress
3 spring onions	3 scallions
300 ml/½ pint soured cream	1¼ cups sour cream
2 teaspoons powdered gelatine	2 teaspoons powdered gelatine
2 tablespoons water	2 tablespoons water
salt and freshly milled black pepper	salt and freshly milled black pepper
To garnish:	To garnish:
watercress leaves	watercress leaves
4 slices of lemon	4 slices of lemon

Put the watercress and spring onions (scallions) into a blender or food processor and chop finely. Add the cream and whizz again. Sprinkle the gelatine (gelatin) over the water in a cup and leave to soften for five minutes, then stand in a pan of simmering water until the gelatine has dissolved. Add to the watercress mixture and mix well, then pour into four ramekin dishes. Chill for at least one hour or until set. Garnish each ramekin with a few watercress leaves and a twist of lemon before serving.

Serves 4 as a starter

Smith Salad

This is an Australian recipe. I have never been able to ascertain who Smith was, but he or she certainly knew how to make a good salad. A salad like this very useful if you have a number of people to lunch – you can make a large bowl of it and it really is a complete meal in itself.

METRIC/IMPERIAL
1 small cauliflower
1 round lettuce heart
1 small cos lettuce
2 heads chicory
1 small bunch watercress
100 g/4 oz sliced salami
100 g/4 oz Gruyère cheese
50 g/1¾ oz can anchovy fillets
150 ml/¼ pint French dressing
  made with olive oil (page 5)

AMERICAN
1 small cauliflower
1 round lettuce heart
1 small cos lettuce
2 heads chicory
1 small bunch watercress
4 oz sliced salami
4 oz Swiss cheese
1¾ oz can anchovy fillets
⅝ cup French dressing made with
  olive oil (page 5)

Break the cauliflower into florets, wash the lettuces, dry well, then shred them, slice the chicory and chop the watercress, discarding the ends of the stalks. Slice the salami and the cheese into matchstick strips and cut the anchovy fillets in half lengthways. Put all the salad ingredients, salami, anchovy fillets and cheese into a salad bowl. Pour over the French dressing and toss the salad about 15 minutes before serving.

Serves 6

Green Salad with Avocado and Banana

A very simple salad, but the combination of flavours works well.

METRIC/IMPERIAL
1 lettuce
1 small bunch waterccress
6 tablespoons French dressing
  made with grape seed or
  sunflower oil (page 5)
1 banana
1 avocado

AMERICAN
1 lettuce
1 small bunch watercress
6 tablespoons French dressing
  made with grape seed or
  sunflower oil (page 5)
1 banana
1 avocado

Wash and dry the lettucce and watercress and put into a salad bowl. Pour the French dressing into a basin. Peel the banana and slice into the dressing, then halve the avocado, stone and peel it and slice this into the dressing. Leave in the dressing until just before serving, then add to the lettuce and toss lightly together.

Serves 4

Mixed Sprout Salad with Tahina Dressing

There is enough protein, vitamins, and minerals in sprouting vegetables so that a variety of them is capable of sustaining life with no other contributing form of food. They are extremely simple to grow yourself and a variety of seeds can be used including alfalfa, aduki beans, chick peas, soya beans, mung beans and sunflower seeds, to name but a few.

The two kinds, however, which are most frequently available in the shops are alfalfa, which to look at closely resemble the mustard and cress one grew as a child, and mung bean sprouts which are, of course, the basis for so many Chinese dishes. They can be served with a variety of different dressings and sauces, but I find they blend especially well with the thick tahina and yogurt on page 14.

METRIC/IMPERIAL	AMERICAN
100 g/4 oz bean sprouts	4 oz bean sprouts
100 g/4 oz alfalfa sprouts	4 oz alfalfa sprouts
1 small red pepper	1 small red pepper
100 g/4 oz mooli	4 oz mooli
5 tablespoons tahina and yogurt (page 14)	5 tablespoons tahina and yogurt (page 14)

Wash the sprouts in cold water and dry thoroughly. Halve the pepper, remove the core and seeds and slice thinly. Peel the mooli and cut into thin slices.

Put all the ingredients together into a bowl and mix well, then turn into a serving dish. As all the ingredients are very juicy, it is not necessary to add extra water to the dressing before adding it to the salad.

Serves 4

Tabboulé

This salad made from crushed wheat and chopped herbs has become increasingly popular over the last few years. Although you can chop the herbs in a blender or food processor, I was assured by the Lebanese owner of a delicatessen in Sydney, that in order to have the correct texture (chopped, rather than minced), it is better to chop the herbs by hand.

METRIC/IMPERIAL
100 g/4 oz crushed wheat or
  burghul
2 tablespoons finely chopped spring
  onions
6 tablespoons chopped parsley
6 tablespoons chopped mint
2 tablespoons olive oil
2 tablespoons lemon juice
salt and freshly milled black
  pepper
To garnish:
black olives
sliced tomatoes

AMERICAN
1 cup crushed wheat or bulgur
2 tablespoons finely chopped
  scallions
6 tablespoons chopped parsley
6 tablespoons chopped mint
2 tablespoons olive oil
2 tablespoons lemon juice
salt and freshly milled black
  pepper
To garnish:

blackolives
sliced tomatoes

Put the crushed wheat or bulgur into a bowl and cover with cold water. Leave for 30 minutes, during which time it will expand. Drain, then wrap in a tea towel and wring out to remove as much moisture as possible. Put into a bowl and add the spring onions (scallions), parsley, mint, oil and lemon juice. Season to taste with salt and pepper. Turn into a serving dish and garnish with black olives and sliced tomatoes.

Creole Achards

An interesting vegetable hors d'oeuvre which can be made using any mixture of raw vegetables you like: French beans, carrots, onions, cauliflower, cabbage, peas, mange tout, red and green peppers, young turnips, kohlrabi, etc. Choose at least three different vegetables with a good range of colours.

METRIC/IMPERIAL	AMERICAN
1½ tablespoons salt	1½ tablespoons salt
1.2 litres/2 pints water	5 cups water
650 g/1½ lb mixed raw vegetables (see above)	1½ lb mixed raw vegetables (see above)
1 medium-sized onion	1 medium-sized onion
a good pinch of saffron powder	a good pinch of saffron powder
¼ teaspoon freshly milled black pepper	¼ teaspoon freshly milled black pepper
¼–½ teaspoon chilli powder	¼–½ teaspoon chilli powder
a good pinch ground cumin	a good pinch ground cumin
150 ml/¼ pint olive oil	⅝ cup olive oil

Dissolve the salt in the water. Prepare the vegetables according to kind: string and chop the beans, peel and dice the carrots, break the cauliflower into florets, shred the cabbage, etc. Put each vegetable into a separate basin and cover with some of the brine. Leave to soak for 24 hours, then drain and dry and place in mounds in a shallow dish.

Peel and finely chop the onion, and put with the saffron, black pepper, chilli powder (chilli powder varies considerably in strength, so the amount required will depend upon personal taste, plus the strength of the powder), cumin and a good pinch of salt into a saucepan with the oil. Bring to the boil, then pour over the vegetables. Cover the dish and leave in a cool place or in the fridge for 24 to 48 hours. Baste the vegetables with the marinade from time to time.

Serves 6

Broad Beans with Basil

You need to have an enormous amount of patience to make this recipe as you either have to use very tiny beans, or if using larger beans, you must peel off the outer sheath so that all you eat are the two halves of the bean which are inside. The end result, however, is well worth the effort.

METRIC/IMPERIAL	AMERICAN
1.35k g/3 lb broad beans	3 lb broad beans
1 red pepper	1 red pepper
150 ml/¼ pint soured cream	⅝ cup sour cream
1 tablespoon wine vinegar	1 tablespoon wine vinegar
3 sprigs basil	3 sprigs basil
salt and freshly milled black pepper	salt and freshly milled black pepper
To garnish:	To garnish:
sprigs of basil	sprigs of basil

Shell the beans (see above) and place in a basin. Dice the pepper, discarding the core and seeds and add to the beans. Blend the cream with the vinegar. Chop the basil, discarding any tough stalks add to the dressing, then pour over the beans and pepper. Season to taste with salt and freshly milled black pepper, and garnish with a few extra sprigs of basil.

Serves 4

Broccoli and Carrot Salad

The contrast in colour between the dark green broccoli and the carrot makes this very simple salad look very spectacular.

METRIC/IMPERIAL	AMERICAN
450 g/1 lb broccoli	1 lb broccoli
225 g/8 oz carrots	8 oz carrots
4 tablespoons mayonnaise (page 6)	4 tablespoons mayonnaise (page 6)
2 tablespoons natural yogurt	2 tablespoons natural yogurt
1½ teaspoons caraway or fennel seed	1½ teaspoons caraway or fennel seed
salt and freshly milled black pepper	salt and freshly milled black pepper

Break the broccoli into very small florets, discarding all the tough, thick stalks. Peel the carrots and cut into sticks about ¼ inch (0.75 cm) thick and 2 inches (5 cm) long. Arrange the carrots and broccoli in a serving dish.

Blend the mayonnaise with the yogurt, stir in the caraway or fennel and season to taste with salt and pepper. Spoon the dressing over the centre of the salad.

Serves 4

Slovakian Salad

Although this is a Czech recipe, they serve a very similar salad with almost every meal in Hungary as well – in fact when they say 'salad' this is what they mean.

METRIC/IMPERIAL	AMERICAN
450g/1 lb sauerkraut	1 lb sauerkraut

225 g/8 oz carrots	8 oz carrots
1 small green pepper	1 small green pepper
1 small onion	1 small onion
4 tablespoons safflower or sunflower oil	4 tablespoons safflower or sunflower oil
1 ½ teaspoons sugar	1 ½ teaspoons sugar
salt and frshly milled black pepper	salt and freshly milled black pepper

Drain the sauerkraut, peel and grate the carrots, de-seed and thinly slice the pepper and peel and finely chop the onion. Combine all these ingredients in a salad bowl, pour over the oil and sprinkle with the sugar. Toss all the ingredients together and season to taste with salt and pepper. Cover and leave to stand for two to three hours before serving, for the flavours to infuse.

Serves 4–6

Red Cabbage Salad

This is a Jewish recipe, which makes a very colourful salad for a buffet party.

METRIC/IMPERIAL	AMERICAN
1 grapefruit	1 grapefruit
1 small kohlrabi	1 small kohlrabi
6 spring onions	6 scallions
1 green pepper	1 green pepper
50 g/2 oz hazelnuts	½ cup hazelnuts
450 g/1 lb red cabbage	1 lb red cabbage
½ small pineapple	½ small pineapple
300 ml/½ pint mayonnaise	1 ¼ cups mayonnaise
salt and freshly milled black pepper	salt and freshly milled black pepper

Peel the grapefruit, removing all the white pith, then cut into segments, discarding all the pith and skin. Do this over the salad bowl so that none of the juice is lost. Put the grapefruit segments into the salad bowl. Peel and grate the kohlrabi, finely chop the spring onions (scallions), de-seed and chop the pepper, chop the hazelnuts, finely shred the red cabbage and cut the pineapple into pieces, discarding all the eyes and the core.

Pile all the ingredients into a salad bowl, together with the mayonnaise and mix well. Season to taste with salt and pepper and leave for 30 minutes before serving, to allow the flavours to infuse.

Serves 6–8

Carrots with Anchovies and Capers

Tubes of anchovy purée, which are only anchovies and salt, invaluable as they keep for months in the fridge and it means you can add anchovy flavour without having to open a can, the remains of which are often wasted.

METRIC/IMPERIAL	AMERICAN
450 g/1 lb carrots	1 lb carrots
4 teaspoons anchovy purée	4 teaspoons anchovy purée
4 tablespoons thick mayonnaise (page 6)	4 tablespoons thick mayonnaise (page 6)
3 tablespoons single cream	3 tablespoons light cream
3 teaspoons capers	3 teaspoons capers
salt and freshly milled black pepper	salt and freshly milled black pepper
To garnish:	To garnish:
1 teaspoon capers	1 teaspoon capers

Coarsely grate the carrots and put into a bowl. Blend the anchovy purée into the mayonnaise, then stir in the cream, capers and seasoning. Pour over the carrots and toss lightly together, then turn into a serving dish and garnish with the extra capers.

Serves 4

Spiced Cauliflower Salad

I find garam masala extremely useful as a flavouring with its combination of different spices, and it is best when slightly 'chunky' containing, for example, a few whole cumin seeds.

METRIC/IMPERIAL	AMERICAN
1 small cauliflower	1 small cauliflower
1 clove of garlic	1 clove of garlic
6 tablespoons French dressing made with sunflower oil (page 6)	6 tablespoons French dressing made with sunflower oil (page 6)
1 tablespoon garam masala	1 tablespoon garam masala
2 tablespoons chopped coriander	2 tablespoons chopped coriander
salt	salt

Break the cauliflower into florets and place in a bowl. Crush the garlic, combine with all the other ingredients and pour over the cauliflower. Toss well together, and taste and adjust the seasoning. Leave to marinate for at least one hour, but for not more than three hours before serving.

Serves 4

Celeriac with Apple

Celeriac is an excellent winter salad vegetable as it has plenty of flavour and is very filling. This salad also has the advantage that it will keep for a couple of days covered in the fridge.

METRIC/IMPERIAL
juice of 1 large orange
150 ml/¼ pint natural yogurt
450 g/1 lb celeriac
2 dessert apples
3 medium-sized dill cucumbers
2 tablespoons chopped parsley
salt and freshly milled black
  pepper

AMERICAN
juice of 1 large orange
⅝ cup natural yogurt
1 lb celeriac
2 dessert apples
3 medium-sized dill pickles
2 tablespoons chopped parsley
salt and freshly milled black
  pepper

Blend the orange juice with the yogurt in a bowl. Peel the celeriac and grate coarsely. Add to the yogurt immediately, to prevent discolouration and mix well. Quarter the apples, core and chop them, add to the celeriac and mix well. Slice the cucumbers (pickles) and add, together with the parsley and seasoning. Turn into a serving dish.

Serves 4–6

Courgette (Zucchini) and Watermelon Salad

This salad really needs to be made up just before serving, or you will find that the dressing will become very liquid. However, if you wish to prepare it earlier, the lettuce can be shredded and the courgettes (zucchini) and watermelon put into a bowl, ready for the yogurt to be added.

METRIC/IMPERIAL
1 large lettuce heart
900 g/2 lb piece of watermelon
450 g/1 lb courgettes
300 ml/½ pint natural yogurt
salt and freshly milled black
  pepper

AMERICAN
1 large lettuce heart
2 lb piece of watermelon
1 lb zucchini
1¼ cups natural yogurt
salt and freshly milled black
  pepper

Shred the lettuce and place in the base of a serving dish. Cut the melon into 1.25 cm/½ inch cubes, discarding the seeds, and place in a bowl. Cut the courgettes (zucchini) into thin slices and add to the melon. Stir in the yogurt and season to taste with salt and pepper. Pile on top of the lettuce and serve as soon as possible.

Serves 4

Japanese Cucumber Salad with Sesame Seeds

Salting the cucumber not only draws out the excess liquid, but reduces any bitterness in the skin.

METRIC/IMPERIAL	AMERICAN
1 *large cucumber*	1 *large cucumber*
1 *teaspoon salt*	1 *teaspoon salt*
3 *tablespoons vinegar*	3 *tablespoons vinegar*
2 *tablespoons sugar*	2 *tablespoons sugar*
2 *tablespoons soy sauce*	2 *tablespoons soy sauce*
1 *tablespoon sesame seeds*	1 *tablespoon sesame seeds*

Cut the unpeeled cucumber into very thin slices. Put into a colander, sprinkle with salt, then stand a plate on the top to press out the liquid. Leave for 30 minutes, then dry well and place in a serving dish. Mix the vinegar, sugar, and soy sauce together and pour over the cucumber just before serving. Toss together, then sprinkle over the sesame seeds.

Serves 4–6

Cucumber with Strawberries

A very attractive summer salad, which is dressed with strawberry liqueur, although this could be replaced with a tablespoon of sweet vermouth or sherry if you prefer.

113

METRIC/IMPERIAL	AMERICAN
1 *medium-sized cucumber*	1 *medium-sized cucumber*
225 g/8 oz strawberries	8 oz strawberries
4 *tablespoons sunflower oil*	4 *tablespoons sunflower oil*
2 *tablespoons wine vinegar*	2 *tablespoons wine vinegar*
1 *tablespoon Fraise des Bois*	1 *tablespoon Fraise des Bois*
liqueur	*liqueur*
salt and freshly milled black	*salt and freshly milled black*
pepper	*pepper*
To garnish:	To garnish:
2 *tablespoons chopped parsley*	2 *tablespoons chopped parsley*

Slice the cucumber and cut the strawberries into slices. If you have plenty of time, arrange them on a large platter, but if not, mix them lightly together and put into a serving dish. Combine the oil, vinegar, liqueur and seasoning in a screw-topped jar. Shake well. Pour over the salad just before serving and sprinkle with the parsley.

Serves 4–6

Kohlrabi with Watercress Sauce

Although you can make this salad up a few hours before you wish to serve it, you will find that some of the juice runs out of the kohlrabi into the sauce, so it will need to be stirred well before serving.

METRIC/IMPERIAL	AMERICAN
4 *tablespoons mayonnaise*	4 *tablespoons mayonnaise*
4 *tablespoons soured cream*	4 *tablespoons sour cream*
1 *small bunch watercress*	1 *small bunch watercress*
salt and freshly milled black	*salt and freshly milled black*
pepper	*pepper*
450 g/1 lb kohlrabi	1 lb kohlrabi

Blend the mayonnaise with the cream. Finely chop the watercress, add to the sauce and season to taste with salt and pepper, adding a little more salt than you think may be necessary as the kohlrabi absorbs the salt. Peel the kohlrabi, cut in half, then cut into thin slices. Add to the watercress and mix lightly, together, then turn into a serving dish.

Serves 4

Mushroom and Mange Tout (Snow Pea) Salad

Freshly chopped herbs really do make all the difference to a salad like this and many of them will flourish throughout the year if kept inside in a warm, sunny place.

METRIC/IMPERIAL	AMERICAN
225 g/8 oz button mushrooms	8 oz button mushrooms
50 g/2 oz mange tout	2 oz snow peas
150 ml/¼ pint mayonnaise (page 6)	⅝ cup mayonnaise (page 6)
4 tablespoons soured cream	4 tablespoons sour cream
1 tablespoon chopped parsley	1 tablespoon chopped parsley
1 tablespoon chopped tarragon	1 tablespoon chopped tarragon
1 tablespoon chopped chives	1 tablespoon chopped chives
salt and freshly milled black pepper	salt and freshly milled black pepper
To garnish:	To garnish:
1 tablespoon chopped chives	1 tablespoon chopped chives

Wipe the mushrooms and slice. String the mange tout (snow peas) and cut each one into about 6 pieces. Put into a bowl with the mushrooms. Add the mayonnaise, cream, herbs and seasoning, and mix well. Turn into a serving dish and leave if possible for about 30 minutes to allow the flavours to infuse.

Serves 4

Mushroom Salad with Soy Sauce

This is one of my favourite mushroom salad recipes, not least of all because it only takes minutes to prepare.

METRIC/IMPERIAL	AMERICAN
450 g/1 lb button mushrooms	1 lb button mushrooms
salt and freshly milled black pepper	salt and freshly milled black pepper
2 teaspoons Worcestershire sauce	2 teaspoons Worcestershire sauce
1 tablespoon soy sauce	1 tablespoon soy sauce

Wipe the mushrooms and leave whole if very small, or else cut into halves or quarters. Put into a serving bowl and season with salt and pepper. Sprinkle over the Worcestershire and soy sauces and blend well. Cover and chill for at least two hours before serving, turning the mushrooms from time to time.

Serves 6

Onion Salad

Onions are frequently blanched in boiling water to make them a little 'gentler' to eat in salads, but the same effect can be achieved by salting them.

METRIC/IMPERIAL	AMERICAN
3–4 large Spanish onions	3–4 large Spanish onions
4 tablespoons salt	4 tablespoons salt
1 teaspoon vinegar	1 teaspoon vinegar
2 tablespoons lemon juice	2 tablespoons lemon juice
2 teaspoons cold water	2 teaspoons cold water
freshly milled black pepper	freshly milled black pepper
3 tablespoons olive oil	3 tablespoons olive oil
1 tablespoon chopped parsley	1 tablespoon chopped parsley

Peel the onion and cut in half lengthwise. Slice each half very thinly. Place the sliced onions in a sieve and sprinkle with the salt. Press the onions and salt together until all the salt has dissolved, then rinse the onions thoroughly under cold running water, drain and dry well.

Mix together the vinegar, lemon juice and water in a salad bowl, and season with pepper. Whisk in the olive oil gradually, add the onion slices and parsley and mix thoroughly. Leave to stand for a few minutes before serving.

Serves 4

Greek Orange and Olive Salad

Greek olives, which are usually mixed with crushed coriander seeds, have a very distinctive flavour and texture. If you wish, a little crumbled feta cheese could also be sprinkled over this salad.

METRIC/IMPERIAL	AMERICAN
4 large oranges	4 large oranges
100 g/4 oz Greek black olives	1 cup Greek black olives
1 tablespoon very finely chopped onion	1 tablespoon very finely chopped onion
4 tablespoons olive oil	4 tablespoons olive oil
2 tablespoons lemon juice	2 tablespoons lemon juice
salt and freshly milled black pepper	salt and freshly milled black pepper

Peel the oranges, discarding all the white pith and skin, and cut into segments; do this over a basin so that you catch any juice. Stone the olives. Put the orange segments, olives and onion into a salad bowl. Put all the remaining ingredients, and any orange juice, into a screw-topped jar and shake until well blended. Pour over the oranges and olives and toss well. Leave for one hour before serving.

Serves 4

Peas with Chervil

Although all peas are always best when they are very sweet and tender, this is essential if you want to eat them raw, so unless they are your home-grown ones, don't buy them unless you can first taste a few of them just to make sure they are all right.

METRIC/IMPERIAL
900 g/2 lb peas
2 rounded tablespoons chopped
    chervil
5 tablespoons French dressing
    made with sunflower oil (page
    5)
freshly milled black pepper

AMERICAN
2 lb peas
2 rounded tablespoons chopped
    chervil
5 tablespoons French dressing
    made with sunflower oil (page
    5)
freshly milled black pepper

Shell the peas, toss with the chervil in the French dressing and season with pepper. Leave to marinate for at least one hour before serving if possible.

Serves 4

Pear and Spinach Salad

Although you ideally want to use walnut oil for this recipe as it combines so well with the pears and spinach, failing that use olive oil and 25 g/1 oz/¼ cup chopped walnuts.

METRIC/IMPERIAL
225 g/8 oz young spinach leaves
2 ripe pears
juice ½ a lemon
1 red pepper
3 tablespoons walnut oil

AMERICAN
8 oz young spinach leaves
2 ripe pears
juice ½ a lemon
1 red pepper
3 tablespoons walnut oil

1 teaspoon French mustard
a pinch of sugar
salt and freshly milled black pepper

1 teaspoon French mustard
a pinch of sugar
salt and freshly milled black pepper

Remove the stalks of the spinach, wash the leaves, then dry thoroughly and tear them into small pieces. Peel, core and dice the pears. Put into a bowl with the lemon juice and toss lightly together, then strain off the liquor into a screw-topped jar. Finely shred the pepper, discarding the core and seeds, and add to the pears. Mix the lemon juice with the walnut oil, mustard, sugar and seasoning in the jar and shake well. Shortly before serving, add the spinach to the pears and pepper, pour over the dressing and toss well together.

Serves 4

Spinach and Chinese Cabbage

Young spinach leaves are one of the very best green salad stuffs, not only in terms of flavour, but also nutritionally, being very high in iron, calcium and Vitamin A.

METRIC/IMPERIAL
100 g/4 oz young spinach leaves
225 g/8 oz Chinese cabbage
100 g/4 oz button mushrooms
5 tablespoons Oriental dressing
  (page 8)
2 tablespoons sunflower seeds

AMERICAN
4 oz young spinach leaves
8 oz Chinese cabbage
4 oz button mushrooms
5 tablespoons Oriental dressing
  (page 8)
2 tablespoons sunflower seeds

Wash and dry the spinach leaves, discarding all the stalks. Tear into pieces and place in a salad bowl. Shred the Chinese leaves, slice the mushrooms and add to the spinach. Pour over the French dressing just before serving, toss lightly together, then sprinkle with the sunflower seeds.

Serves 4

Sprout Slaw

You want to have a really good, thick mayonnaise for this slaw, as kohlrabi is a very juicy vegetable.

METRIC/IMPERIAL	AMERICAN
350 g/12 oz Brussels sprouts	12 oz Brussels sprouts
1 small leek	1 small leek
1 red pepper	1 red pepper
350 g/12 oz kohlrabi	12 oz kohlrabi
75 g/3 oz peanuts	¾ cup peanuts
200 ml/8 fl oz mayonnaise (page 6)	1 cup mayonnaise (page 6)
(1 teaspoon cumin seeds	1 teaspoon cumin seeds
salt and freshly milled black pepper	salt and freshly milled black pepper

Discard the outer leaves of the sprouts and shred them finely. Finely shred the leek discarding the outer sheath and both ends and cut the pepper into fine dice, discarding the core and seeds. Peel and coarsely grate the kohlrabi. Put all the vegetables into a bowl with the peanuts. Add the mayonnaise and cumin seeds and mix well. Season to taste, then turn into a serving dish.

Serves 6–8

Tomato and Kiwi Fruit Salad with Ginger

A simple salad which goes well with delicate mousses or similar main courses, and looks stunningly pretty.

METRIC/IMPERIAL	AMERICAN
450 g/1 lb tomatoes	1 lb tomatoes

2 *kiwi fruit*
salt and freshly milled black
  pepper
juice ½ a lime
1 *tablespoon very finely chopped*
  ginger
2 *tablespoond chopped chives*

2 *kiwi fruit*
salt and freshly milled black
  pepper
juice ½ a lime
1 *tablespoon very finely chopped*
  ginger
2 *tablespoons chopped chives*

Slice the tomatoes and peel and slice the kiwi fruit. Arrange them both attractively on a large platter. Season with salt and pepper and sprinkle over the lime juice, then scatter the ginger and chives evenly over the top. Cover with clingwrap until ready to serve, but do not prepare more than about an hour before serving.

Serves 4

FRUIT AND DESSERTS

The desserts in this chapter can be divided into two categories – fruit salads; and those made generally with fruit as well, but also with some form of dairy produce, either yogurt, cream or cheese. Using cream may cause a little head-shaking on the part of some pundits, but I feel that if you are eating a sensible, well-balanced diet, there is no reason why you should not eat what is a totally natural product from time to time. Unquestionably, fresh fruit served either on its own or as a fruit salad, is one of the simplest, healthiest and most delicious desserts one can have, but we all need (and enjoy) a change from time to time. If you are really concerned about using cream, however, in some recipes it could be replaced with yogurt, or one of the new low-fat cream substitutes based on buttermilk and vegetable oil.

Air transport gives us a vast range of fresh fruit available throughout the year, so we are not, as our grandmothers were, restricted to apples and pears, enlivened by the odd orange and banana throughout the winter months. As with vegetables, it is important to choose fruit that has a good flavour, so one still finds the best apples in the autumn and the best strawberries and raspberries in the height of summer – quite apart from the rather important fact that they are cheaper at these times of year.

Dried fruits are also highly nutritious. While new methods have been found for preserving them so that they are more tender and moist, *some* (not all) of these require the use of chemicals for preservation. Until more is known about the long-term effects these can have on the body, I feel fruits preserved in this way should be avoided, as should those that look very shiny and glistening, as they have usually been tossed in mineral oil. I therefore like to buy mine from a health food store where, hopefully, they do not sell products that have been subjected to these processes.

Although there is no denying that certain health food stores charge exhorbitant prices for things like dried fruit and nuts, there are others, possibly run for more altruistic reasons, where the prices are considerably cheaper than they are in the larger supermarkets. I have also noticed that some open country markets also have a health food stall, and these often represent very good value for money as well.

The nutritional value of nuts, not surprisingly, varies considerably with the type, but the majority of them have a very high protein content. The greatest amount of all is in pine nuts, (which are not technically a nut at all but a seed), which can have as much as 31%, considerably higher than most meats which have only 20%. Peanuts come next in the table with 28%, almonds 20% and walnuts 12%. From this it can be seen why nuts can form such an import part of a vegetarian, and especially a vegan diet.

I have used them throughout the book in a number of different savoury recipes, and in this chapter I have used both almond and hazelnuts bound with a little honey to make flan cases. Any nut you like can be used for this purpose and these healthy substitutes for the more traditional pastry cases are extremely popular. The resulting case can be filled with anything you like from simple fresh fruit to mousses, cheesecakes, and fools, adding an interesting dimension to raw desserts.

Yogurt with Wheatgerm

This was the mainstay of my diet when I spent a weekend at a health farm, and ever since I have been quite addicted to it. They used their own home-made yogurt, which is obviously ideal, but you can use any variety you wish including goat's, cow's and sheep's. They did not actually include the nuts and raisins, but I think they do improve it.

METRIC/IMPERIAL	AMERICAN
150 ml/¼ pint natural yogurt	⅝ cup natural yogurt
1 rounded tablespoon wheatgerm	1 rounded tablespoon wheatgerm
2 teaspoons chopped nuts	2 teaspoons chopped nuts
1 teaspoon raisins	1 teaspoon raisins

Chill the yogurt. Mix the wheatgerm with the nuts and raisins and scatter over the yogurt shortly before serving.

Serves 1

Cream Cheese with Wine

Although you can serve this on its own accompanied by some little crisp biscuits, I think it is really best if it is accompanied by some fresh fruit such as strawberries, cherries or peaches.

METRIC/IMPERIAL	AMERICAN
450 g/1 lb cream cheese	2 cups cream cheese
100 g/4 oz caster sugar (see below)	½ cup superfine sugar (see below)
5 tablespoons white wine	5 tablespoons white wine
juice 1 lemon	juice 1 lemon

Sieve the cheese into a bowl, then beat in the sugar and gradually beat in the wine and lemon juice. Taste the mixture and add a little more sugar if necessary; the amount of sugar required will depend on the type of wine used. Either turn into a serving bowl, or spoon into individual glasses or dishes. Chill for at least two hours before serving.

Serves 4–6

Cinnamon Ice Cream with Orange and Apricot Purée

Cinnamon always makes me think of Christmas, and this would be an ideal dessert for this time of year.

METRIC/IMPERIAL	AMERICAN
For the ice cream	For the ice cream:
4 *egg yolks*	4 *egg yolks*
75 g/3 oz icing sugar	¾ cup confectioners sugar
1 rounded teaspoon ground cinnamon	1 rounded teaspoon ground cinnamon
300 ml/½ pint double cream	1½ cups heavy cream
For the purée:	For the purée:
100 g/4 oz dried apricots	1 cup dried apricots
200 ml/8 fl oz orange juice	1 cup orange juice
To decorate (optional):	To decorate (optional):
25 g/1 oz chopped walnuts	¼ cup chopped walnuts

Whisk the egg yolks, icing sugar and cinnamon together until thick and creamy. Lightly whip the cream until it holds its shape, then fold in the cinnamon mixture. Turn into a container and freeze, removing the mixture from the freezer two or three times and beating well.

For the purée, soak the apricots in the orange juice for 12 hours, then purée in a blender or food processor.

Remove the ice cream from the freezer and leave to soften for about 10 minutes at room temperature, or 30 minutes in the refrigerator. Pile scoopfuls into individual dishes and spoon over some of the sauce and sprinkle with the chopped nuts if wished.

Serves 4–6

Caribbean Fruit Salad

Coconut liqueur gives this very simple fruit salad the authentic taste of the Caribbean, but it could be replaced with three tablespoons white rum and a tablespoon of grated coconut, preferably fresh, but desiccated could be used.

METRIC/IMPERIAL	AMERICAN
1 medium-sized pineapple	1 medium-sized pineapple
5 tablespoons coconut liqueur	5 tablespoons cocconut liqueur
2 large bananas	2 large bananas

Reserve the leaves of the pineapple for decorating, then peel the pineapple, removing all the eyes. Cut it in half and remove the core, then cut into pieces, saving all the juice. Add the coconut liqueur, cover and leave for at least one hour, or for up to six. Peel and slice the banana, add to the pineapple and mix well, then turn into a serving dish and decorate with the reserved pineapple leaves.

Serves 4–6

Tropical Fruit Salad with Nasturtium Flowers

Decorating this fruit salad with nasturtium flowers, (which one can buy in some supermarkets, or pick from your garden), whilst obviously not essential, does make it look as exotic as it tastes. The exact constituents of the salad can be varied, depending on what is available, but it is very important with tropical fruit that they are really ripe, as it is only then that their true flavour comes out. Mangoes, pawpaws (papayas), guavas and pineapples should be soft to the touch and a good yellow/orange, depending on the fruit and the variety. Passion-fruit must be slightly wrinkled; the beautiful, smooth ones are under-ripe and can be quite sharp.

METRIC/IMPERIAL	AMERICAN
1 ripe mango	1 ripe mango
1 ripe pawpaw	1 ripe pawpaw
2 ripe guavas	2 ripe guavas

1 *small ripe pineapple*	1 *small ripe pineapple*
4–6 ripe passion-fruit	*4–6 ripe passion-fruit*
To decorate:	To decorate:
nasturtium flowers	*nasturtium flowers*

As all these fruit are very juicy, it is best to peel them over a bowl so that you do not waste any of the juice. Peel the mango, scoop out the flesh from the skin and put in a bowl, then cut the flesh from the mango into slices and discard the stone. Halve the paw paw and scoop out the seeds (these can be used to make an excellent dressing, see page 7). Peel and cut the flesh into cubes. Peel the guavas, then cut across the slices. Cut off the top and base of the pineapple, and peel the fruit, removing all the eyes. Cut in half and take out the core, then dice the flesh. Cut the passion-fruit in half with a sharp knife and scoop out the pulp with a teaspoon. Put all the fruit, together with all the juice into a large serving bowl and decorate with the nasturtium flowers.

Arabian Flan

Unblanched almonds and dates make an excellent raw flan case and combine well with the oranges. If you wish, the oranges can be soaked in a little orange flower water for 30 minutes before being added to the flan.

METRIC/IMPERIAL	AMERICAN
For the crust:	For the crust:
225 g/8 oz unblanched almonds	2 cups unblanched almonds
175 g/6 oz dried dates	¾ cup dried dates
3 tablespoons honey	3 tablespoons honey
For the filling:	For the filling:
4 oranges	4 oranges
300 ml/½ pint double cream	1¼ cups heavy cream

Put the almonds into a blender or food processor and whizz until they are almost smooth. Add the dates and whizz again until they are quite finely chopped, then add the honey and whizz again. Press the mixture into a 20 cm/8 inch flan dish and chill while preparing the filling.

Finely grate the rind of two of the oranges and add to the cream in a bowl. Peel the oranges, discarding all the white pith and cut across into slices. Whip the cream and orange rind until it holds its shape, then spread half of it over the base of the flan dish. Cover with the oranges, reserving about three slices for decoration, then cover with the remaining cream. Decorate the top with the reserved orange slices and chill until ready to serve.

Serves 6–8

Hazelnut Flan with Raspberry Fool

Raspberries and cream are frequently used to sandwich together hazelnut meringues or in a hazelnut torte, and in this recipe, ground hazelnuts are mixed with honey to make a 'raw' flan case.

METRIC/IMPERIAL	AMERICAN
225 g/8 oz hazelnuts	2 cups hazelnuts
2 tablespoons clear honey	2 tablespoons clear honey
1 tablespoon lemon juice	1 tablespoon lemon juice
350 g/12 oz raspberries	12 oz raspberries
50 g/2 oz soft brown sugar	1/3 cup soft brown sugar
300 ml/1/2 pint double cream	1 1/4 cups heavy cream

Coarsely grind the hazelnuts in a blender or food processor, then add the honey and lemon juice and quickly whizz again so that they are blended. Press the nuts into the base of a 20 cm/8 inch flan dish to make a base and chill while preparing the filling.

Reserve a few of the best raspberries for decoration and purée the remainder with the sugar. Lightly whip the cream until it holds its shape, then fold in the raspberry purée. Pile into the centre of the flan and decorate with the reserved raspberries. Chill until ready to serve.

Serves 6

Bilberry Pie

One of America's most popular dishes, given a slightly different twist. When I tested it I used a commercial unsweetened muesli made with wheat flakes and a high proportion of fruit and nuts, which was excellent; home-made would probably be better still, but whichever you choose make sure it is a chunky, crunchy type.

METRIC/IMPERIAL	AMERICAN
300 ml/½ pint double cream	1¼ cups heavy cream
450 g/1 lb blueberries	1 lb blueberries
50 g/2 oz caster sugar	¼ cup superfine sugar
2 tablespoons clear honey	2 tablespoons clear honey
225 g/8 oz fruit and nut muesli (see above)	2 cups fruit and muesli (see above)

Whip the cream until it holds its shape, then fold in the blueberries and sugar. Pile into a pie dish. Stir the honey into the muesli in a basin and mix well, then scatter generously over the top of the blueberry mixture to make a 'pie crust'. Chill until ready to serve, but do not prepare more than about an hour before serving, or the muesli mixture will absorb too much moisture from the cream and will become soggy.

Serves 6

Syrian Apples

The unmistakable flavour and scent of rose-water gives this fruit salad a true Middle Eastern flavour.

METRIC/IMPERIAL	AMERICAN
juice 1 lemon	juice 1 lemon
450 g/1 lb dessert apples	1 lb dessert apples
100 g/4 oz fresh dates	4 oz fresh dates
2 tablespoons clear honey	2 tablespoons clear honey
2 tablespoons rose water	2 tablespoons rose water

Pour the lemon juice into a bowl. Core the apples, and chop them into 0.75cm/¼ inch dice. Add to the lemon juice and mix well to prevent them from discolouring. Halve the dates, remove the stones and chop them into pieces about the same size as the apple. Stir in the honey and rose water. Mix well together and chill for at least 30 minutes before serving for the flavours to infuse. Serve with natural yogurt.

Serves 4–6

Samantha's Special

I was not very certain about this reccipe when I tested it, but my elder daughter adored it, so I decided to include it after all.

METRIC/IMPERIAL	AMERICAN
225 g/8 oz black currants	8 oz black currants
2 egg whites	2 egg whites
50 g/2 oz icing sugar	½ cup confectioners sugar
150 ml/¼ pint double cream	⅝ cup heavy cream

Remove all the stalks from the black currants and put the fruit to one side. Whisk the egg whites until they form stiff peaks, then whisk in the sugar a teaspoon at a time. Lightly whip the cream and fold into the egg whites, then fold in the black currants reserving a few for decorating. Pile into individual dishes and decorate with the reserved black currants.

Serves 4

Greek Yogurt with Figs

A simple, but ambrosial, dessert for which it is essential to use Greek yogurt. If you wish, a little Grand Marnier or Cointreau can be poured over the figs.

METRIC/IMPERIAL
8 *ripe figs*
2 *teaspoons honey*
350 g/12 oz pot cow or goat's milk
   yogurt

AMERICAN
8 *ripe figs*
2 *teaspoons honey*
12 oz pot cow or goat's milk yogurt

Cut the figs into slices and arrange in the base of four individual glasses. Blend the honey with the yogurt and spoon over the figs. Chill until ready to serve.

Serves 4

Grapefruit Soufflé

Despite not being a grapefruit fan, I was delighted with this recipe, which makes a perfect, refreshing ending to a meal.

METRIC/IMPERIAL
3 *large grapefruit*
15 g/½ oz or 1 envelope powdered
   gelatine
4 *eggs, separated*
125g/5 oz clear honey

AMERICAN
3 *large grapefruit*
1 *envelope unflavored gelatin*
4 *eggs, separated*
⅝ *cup clear honey*

Peel the grapefruit, discarding all the white pith, then, holding the fruit over a bowl, cut out all the segments, discarding the pith. Squeeze the pith to extract all the juice. Strain the juice off into a small basin and sprinkle with the gelatine (gelatin). Put on one side to soften for five minutes, then stand over a pan of hot water and leave until the gelatine has completely dissolved.

Whisk the egg yolks with the honey until the mixture is thick and creamy, then beat in the grapefruit juice and gelatine. Put on one side until the mixture is beginning to thicken, then whisk well and stir in the grapefruit segments.

Whisk the egg whites until they form stiff peaks, then fold into the grapefruit mixture. Turn into a serving bowl and chill for one hour or until set.

Serves 4–6

Ginger Wine and Kiwi Fruit Syllabub

Ginger wine, which is probably used most frequently added to whisky as a 'Whisky Mac', is excellent in both sweet and savoury dishes.

METRIC/IMPERIAL	AMERICAN
4 kiwi fruit	4 kiwi fruit
150 ml/¼ pint double cream	⅝ cup heavy cream
2 egg whites	2 egg whites
4 tablespoons ginger wine	4 tablespoons ginger wine
25 g/1 oz caster sugar	⅛ cup superfine sugar

Peel the kiwi fruit, cut them into slices and place in the bottom of four glasses, reserving four slices for decoration. Put the cream, egg whites, ginger wine and sugar into a bowl. Using an electric beater, on slow speed to start with, whisk the mixture until it stands in soft peaks. Spoon the syllabub mixture on top of the fruit, then decorate with the reserved slices. Chill for at least 30 minutes before serving, but do not leave for more than about four hours or the mixture will start to separate.

Serves 4

Kiwi Cream

Kiwi fruit, or Chinese gooseberries as they used to be known, have become increasingly popular and more easily available over the last few years.

METRIC/IMPERIAL	AMERICAN
6 kiwi fruit	6 kiwi fruit
4 tablespoons kirsch	4 tablespoons kirsch
75 g/3 oz demerara sugar	½ cup demerara sugar
200 ml/½ pint double cream	1¼ cups heavy cream
300 ml/½ pint natural yogurt	1¼ cups natural yogurt

Peel the kiwi fruit and cut into slices. Put into a basin, pour over the kirsch and sprinkle with half the sugar. Leave to macerate for about one hour.

Whip the cream until it forms soft peaks, then fold in the yogurt. Put a layer of the cream mixture into the base of six glasses. Divide the kiwi fruit, together with the juices and macerating liqueur, between the glasses, then cover with a second layer of cream. Sprinkle the remaining sugar over the top and chill for one to two hours before serving.

Serves 6

Melon with Red Currants

Although you could serve this as a dessert, I think it is really best as a starter.

METRIC/IMPERIAL	AMERICAN
1 medium-sized Ogen, Charentais or similar sweet melon	1 medium-sized Ogen, Charentais or similar sweet melon
50 g/2 oz red currants	2 oz red currants

1 *tablespoon icing sugar*
1 *tablespoon chopped mint*
To garnish:
sprigs of fresh mint

1 *tablespoon confectioners' sugar*
1 *tablespoon chopped mint*
To garnish:
sprigs of fresh mint

Halve the melon and remove the seeds. Peel off the skin and dice the flesh into one inch cubes. Put into a basin. String the red currants and add to the melon with the sugar and mint. Cover and chill for one hour. Turn into a serving bowl and decorate with fresh mint.

Serves 4

Individual Grand Marnier Soufflés

Individual soufflés make an impressive end to a dinner party, but you do need *little* ramekins in order to make them, or you will find the portions are rather large. If you prefer you can make this mixture in a 600 ml/1 pint/2½ cup soufflé dish.

METRIC/IMPERIAL	AMERICAN
15 g/½ oz or 1 envelope powdered gelatine	1 envelope unflavoured gelatin
juice 1 orange	juice 1 orange
3 eggs, separated	3 eggs, separated
100 g/4 oz caster sugar	½ cup superfine sugar
grated rind 2 oranges	grated rind 2 oranges
4 tablespoons Grand Marnier	4 tablespoons Grand Marnier
150 ml/¼ pint double cream	⅝ cup heavy cream
150 ml/¼ pint single cream	⅝ cup light cream
To decorate:	To decorate:
1 orange	1 orange

Ideally use non-stick silicone baking parchment, or failing that greaseproof paper. Cut six pieces of paper large enough to go round small ramekins, of about 75 m/3 fl oz/⅓ cup capacity. Fold the piece of paper in half lengthways and brush with a little butter or oil. Wrap each one round a ramekin dish, so that it stands at least 5 cm/2 inches above the top of the dish and tie in place with string.

Sprinkle the gelatine (gelatin) over the orange juice in a small basin or cup and leave to soften for five minutes, then stand the basin or cup over a pan of gently simmering water and leave until the gelatine has completely dissolved.

Whisk the egg yolks with the sugar and orange rind until the mixture is thick and creamy. Gradually beat in the Grand Marnier, then the dissolved gelatine.

Whip the double (heavy) and single (light) cream together until it holds its shape and fold into the mixture. Whisk the egg whites until they form soft peaks, then fold in. Divide the mixture between the six ramekin dishes and chill for at least two hours or until set.

To serve, remove the string and gently peel back the paper, using a heated spatula if necessary, but if you have used non-stick paper, it will come away easily. Peel the orange, discarding all the white pith, then cut into segments, removing all the skin and pith. Use the segments to decorate the tops of the soufflés.

Serves 6

Orange Malakoff

A truly delicious concoction of ground almonds, oranges, liqueur and cream. If you have the time, there is no doubt that you will achieve an even better flavour if you first blanch and then grind the nuts yourself rather than using ready ground ones.

METRIC/IMPERIAL	AMERICAN
4 large oranges	4 large oranges
175 g/6 oz softened unsalted butter	¾ cup softened sweet butter
	½ cup superfine sugar

100 g/4 oz caster sugar
2 tablespoons Grand Marnier or
   Cointreau
100 g/4 oz ground almonds
2 tablespoons flaked almonds
150 ml/¼ pint double cream
150 ml/¼ pint single cream

2 tablespoons Grand Marnier or
   Cointreau
1 cup ground almonds
2 tablespoons flaked almonds
⅝ cup heavy cream
⅝ cup light cream

Grate the rind from one of the oranges and put into a mixing bowl. Peel the remaining oranges, discarding all the white pith, then cut across into slices, reserving the juice.

Cream together the butter, sugar and orange rind until very light and fluffy. Beat in the Grand Marnier or Cointreau. Strain off all the juice from the oranges and beat this into the creamed mixture alternately with the ground almonds. Fold in the flaked almonds. Whip the double (heavy) and single (light) cream together until stiff, then fold into the almond mixture.

Spoon half the almond mixture into the base of a serving dish. Lay two-thirds of the oranges on top, reserving the best slices for decoration. Cover with the remaining almond mixture, smoothing the top evenly, and decorate with the reserved orange slices. Chill until ready to serve.

Serves 6

Nectarines in Tropical Jelly

A very refreshing dessert made using a commercially-produced tropical fruit juice. These are usually a combination of mango, passion-fruit, pawpaw and pineapple juices, the exact constituents varying from producer to producer. You need to be careful that it does not have too high a proportion of pineapple juice, or you will have difficulty in setting the jelly, and will have to increase the amount of gelatine.

METRIC/IMPERIAL	AMERICAN
600 ml/1 pint tropical fruit juice	2½ cups tropical fruit juice
15 g/½ oz or 1 envelope powdered gelatine	1 envelope unflavored gelatin
2 large ripe nectarines	2 large ripe nectarines

Take out four tablespoons of the fruit juice and put into a cup or small bowl. Sprinkle over the gelatine (gelatin) and leave for five minutes to soften, then stand the basin over a pan of gently simmering water until it has completely dissolved. Remove from the heat and stir into the remaining fruit juice.

Halve the nectarines and remove the stones. Dip the cut side of each nectarine quickly into the liquid jelly, then place, cut side down in a glass, or individual serving bowl. Chill for about 10 minutes or until the nectarine half adheres quite firmly to the glass. Pour over the remaining fruit juice and chill for about two hours or until set.

Serves 4

Rosy Peaches

A simple, but elegant dessert which I have served on summer picnics as it is easy to transport in a plastic container.

METRIC/IMPERIAL	AMERICAN
6 peaches	6 peaches
1 tablespoon lemon juice	1 tablespoon lemon juice
350 g/12 oz raspberries	12 oz raspberries
25 g/1 oz caster sugar	⅛ cup superfine sugar
150 ml/¼ pint double cream	⅝ cup heavy cream

Peel the peaches, halve and stone them. If they are difficult to peel, dip them very quickly into boiling water. Brush each peach half all over with a tiny amount of lemon juice and place in a serving bowl.

Purée the raspberries and sieve them to remove all the pips. Stir in the sugar and leave until it has dissolved, then stir in the cream. Pour over the peaches, cover and chill until ready to serve.

Serves 6

Pineapple Ice Cream with Chocolate Fudge Filling

This is a little bit of a cheat, in that I have used chocolate, which is not really raw, and heated it with some double cream to melt it, but the combination worked out so well that I just had to include it.

METRIC/IMPERIAL	AMERICAN
For the pineapple ice cream:	For the pineapple ice cream:
½ medium-sized pinapple	½ medium-sized pineapple
4 eggs yolks	4 egg yolks
100 g/4 oz caster sugar	½ cup superfine sugar
2 tablespoons kirsch	2 tablespoons kirsch
300 ml/½ pint double cream	1¼ cups heavy cream
For the chocolate fudge:	For the chocolate fudge:
100 g/4 oz plain chocolate	4 squares semi-sweet chocolate
150 ml/¼ pint double cream	⅝ cup heavy cream

Peel the pineapple, removing all the eyes. Cut out the core and chop the flesh roughly, preserving all the juice. Purée the fruit and juice in a blender or food processor.

Whisk the egg yolks and sugar together until thick and creamy, then beat in the pineapple purée and kirsch. Whip the cream until it holds its shape, then fold in the pineapple mixture. Turn into a container. Place in the freezer. When it is beginning to freeze, remove from the freezer and beat well. Spoon into a pudding basin of about 1.2 litres/2 pints (five cup) capacity. Suspend a small basin, or even a mug, of 300 ml/½ 1¼ cup pint capacity in the centre, if necessary, using a few weights to weight it down, and replace in the freezer. Freeze until firm.

Remove from the freezer and take out the small basin or mug; this can sometimes be done by just a little gentle levering, but if not, pour in a little boiling water, leave it for about a minute, then when the ice cream round the edge of it has melted gently remove it. Replace in the freezer.

Break the chocolate into pieces and put into a small pan with the cream. Stand over a very gentle heat and stir well until the chocolate has melted, then remove from the heat and allow to cool for about 10 minutes, stirring it frequently. Pour this mixture into the hole in the centre of the ice cream, then return to the freezer for at least two hours.

To serve the ice cream, dip the bowl quickly into very hot water, then invert it on to a serving plate and remove the bowl. If wished the ice cream can be decorated with the remainder of the pineapple, peeled and cut into slices, and the pineapple leaves.

Serves 6–8

Plums with Kumquats and Vermouth

This idea came to me while standing rather vacantly in the fruit department of a supermarket, and I was really pleased by the way it turned out. As both the kumquats and vermouth are slightly bitter, you do want to choose ripe plums with plenty of flavour.

METRIC/IMPERIAL
450 g/1 lb ripe plums
2 tablespoons soft brown or raw
  sugar
50 g/2 oz kumquats
100 ml/4 fl oz sweet vermouth

AMERICAN
1 lb ripe plums
2 tablespoons soft brown or raw
  sugar
2 oz kumquats
½ cup sweet vermouth

Halve the plums, remove the stones and place them in a serving dish. Sprinkle over the sugar, slice the kumquats thinly and scatter over the plums. Pour over the vermouth. Cover with clingwrap and chill for at least 12 hours or up to 24. Serve with plenty of whipped cream.

Serves 4

Frosted Raspberry Layer

An American recipe for a very light, semi-frosted dessert, which I have found extremely popular with both adults and children. It stores well in the freezer, so it's worth making up a fairly large quantity, although I doubt that you will be keeping it for long!

METRIC/IMPERIAL	AMERICAN
2 egg whites	2 egg whites
2 tablespoons lemon juice	2 tablespoons lemon juice
450 g/1 lb fresh or frozen raspberries, defrosted	1 lb fresh or frozen raspberries, defrosted
225 g/8 oz caster sugar	1 cup superfine sugar
150 ml/¼ pint double cream	⅝ cup heavy cream
150 ml/¼ pint single cream	⅝ cup light cream
225 g/8 oz walnuts	2 cups walnuts
2 tablespoons clear honey	2 tablespoons clear honey

Put the egg whites, lemon juice and most of the raspberries (reserving a few for decoration) into a large bowl. Using an electric mixer, whisk gently and gradually beat in the sugar. Increase the speed to high and whisk for about 10 minutes or until the mixture forms stiff peaks. Whip the double (heavy) and single (light) cream together until stiff, then fold into the raspberry mixture.

Coarsely chop the nuts, put into a basin and stir in the honey. Spoon half the raspberry mixture into the base of a large serving dish (plastic, perspex or other material which will stand freezing is ideal). Sprinkle over the walnuts, then spoon in the remainder of the raspberry mixture. Put into the freezer and freeze for at least six hours. Decorate with the remaining raspberries before serving.

Serves 10–12

Raspberries with Redcurrants

This pretty red fruit salad is a treat simply because there are only a few weeks in the year when both these delectable fruit are in season.

METRIC/IMPERIAL	AMERICAN
225 g/8 oz red currants	8 oz red currants
225 g/8 oz raspberries	8 oz raspberries
about 1 tablespoon caster sugar	about 1 tablespoon superfine sugar
To decorate:	To decorate:
2 tablespoons flaked almonds	2 tablespoons flaked almonds

String the red currants and put into a serving dish with the raspberries. Sprinkle over the sugar, mix lightly together, cover and chill for at least one hour. Scatter with the almonds before serving.

Serves 4

Denork Special

Having spent a number of summers helping friends with their raspberry field in Fife, I genuinely believe that the very best raspberries do come from Scotland, especially the area round the Tay. The reason, it was explained to me, is that raspberries like to have a little rain every day – and in Scotland they usually get it!

METRIC/IMPERIAL	AMERICAN
300 ml/½ pint double cream	1¼ cups heavy cream
3 tablespoons clear honey (a heather honey would be perfect)	3 tablespoons clear honey (a heather honey would be perfect)
3 tablespoons Scotch whisky	3 tablespoons Scotch whisky
2 tablespoons lemon juice	2 tablespoons lemon juice
225 g/8 oz raspberries	8 oz raspberries

Whip the cream until it is stiff. Continue whisking gently and beat in the honey, whisky and lemon juice. Divide half the mixture between four glasses, then scatter over slightly more than half the raspberries. Spoon in the remaining cream and top with the last of the raspberries. Chill until ready to serve.

Serves 4

Redcurrants and Mango with Yogurt

The mango juice combines superbly well with the redcurrants to make a simple but sensational, dessert.

METRIC/IMPERIAL	AMERICAN
1 large mango	1 large mango
100 g/4 oz redcurrants	4 oz redcurrants
350 g/12 oz pot of Greek yogurt	12 oz pot of Greek yogurt

Peel the mango and cut into slices. String the redcurrants, add to the mango, then stir in the yogurt. Turn into a serving bowl and chill lightly.

Serves 4

Strawberries in Mango Purée

If you are dieting but feel that strawberries just aren't strawberries unless they are eaten with lashings of sugar and cream, then this is the recipe for you: despite being a cream devotee, I can promise that it really does not need any.

METRIC/IMPERIAL	AMERICAN
1 lare ripe mango	1 large ripe mango
450 g/1 lb strawberries	1 lb strawberries
a squeeze of lime or lemon juice	a squeeze of lime or lemon juice

Peel the mango and purée the flesh in a blender or food processor. Hull the strawberries and halve them. Add to the mango purée with a squeeze of lime or lemon juice.

Serves 3–4

Strawberries with Pineapple

Obviously the strawberry liqueur teams up well with this mixture, but whatever you happen to have in the cupboard, for example white rum or brandy, could be used instead.

METRIC/IMPERIAL	AMERICAN
350 g/12 oz strawberries	12 oz strawberries
4 tablespoons Fraise des Bois liqueur	4 tablespoons Fraise des Bois liqueur
1 small pineapple	1 small pineapple.

Hull the strawberries, cut them in half and place in a serving bowl. Pour over the liqueur, cover and chill for one hour. Peel the pineapple, discarding all the eyes. Cut it in half and remove the core, then cut into 5 cm/½ inch pieces. Add these to the strawberries, together with any pineapple juice and mix together.

Serves 4

Strawberry Cheesecake

One of the great advantages of serving cheesecake as a dessert is that it is just as popular with children as it is with adults.

METRIC/IMPERIAL

For the crust:
175 g/6 oz ground almonds
50 g/2 oz caster sugar
2–3 tablespoons lemon juice
For the cheesecake:
350 g/12 oz strawberries
350 g/12 oz cottage cheese
15 g/½ oz or 1 envelope powdered
  gelatine
4 tablespoons water
2 eggs, separated
grated rind 1 lemon
75 g/3 oz caster sugar
150 ml/¼ pint double cream
To decorate:
whipped cream
fresh strawberries

AMERICAN

For the crust:
1½ cups ground almonds
¼ cup superfine sugar
2–3 tablespoons lemon juice
For the cheesecake:
12 oz strawberries
1½ cups cottage cheese
1 envelope unflavored gelatin
4 tablespoons water
2 eggs separated
grated rind 1 lemon
⅜ cup superfine sugar
⅝ cup heavy cream
To decorate:
whipped cream
fresh strawberries

Mix the ground almonds with the sugar in a basin. Bind with the lemon juice to form a firm dough. Knead lightly on a surface lightly dusted with icing sugar, then roll out to a 20 cm/8 inch circle. Place in the bottom of a lightly oiled 20 cm/8 inch loose-bottomed cake tin or springform pan.

Purée the strawberries with the cottage cheese in a blender or food processor. Sprinkle the gelatine (gelatin) over the cold water in a basin and put on one side for five minutes to soften, then stand over a pan of gently simmering water until the gelatine has completely dissolved.

Whisk the egg yolks with the lemon rind and sugar until the mixture is thick and creamy, then whisk in the gelatine. Stir in the cheese and strawberry purée. Whip the cream until it holds its shape and whisk the egg whites until they form stiff peaks. Fold first the cream and then the egg whites into the cheesecake mixture. Turn into the cake tin on top of the almond paste and leave to set for at least three hours.

To remove from the tin, loosen the edges of the cheesecake with a knife, then push up the bottom of the tin or simply release the springform pan. Lift carefully on to a serving plate and decorate with whipped cream and a few fresh strawberries.

Serves 8

Apricot Mousse

There are two kinds of dried apricots; the moist, slightly sweet ones, which are a bright orange colour, and the much drier, sharper ones, which are almost brown. You can use either for this dish, but the latter will require 24 hours soaking.

METRIC/IMPERIAL	AMERICAN
225 g/8 oz dried apricots	2 cups dried apricots
200 ml/½ pint water	1¼ cups water
juice 1 lemon	juice 1 lemon
2 teaspoons powdered gelatine	2 teaspoons unflavored gelatin
25–50g/1–2 oz raw sugar	⅙–⅓ cup raw sugar
2 egg whites	2 egg whites
2 tablespoons chopped walnuts	2 tablespoons chopped walnuts

Soak the apricots in the water and half the lemon juice for 12 to 24 hours or until they are very tender. Purée in a blender or food processor, together with the soaking liquor. Sprinkle the gelatine (gelatin) over the remaining lemon juice in a small cup and allow to soften for five minutes. Stand over a pan of hot water and leave until the gelatine has completely dissolved, then add to the apricot purée. Sweeten to taste with sugar. Whisk the egg whites until they form stiff peaks, then fold them into the apricot purée. Divide the mixture between four glasses and chill for one hour, or until set. Sprinkle with the nuts before serving.

Serves 4

Kohshaf

In order for the dried fruit in this salad to become really soft, they need to be soaked for 48 hours. You can use any mixture of dried fruits you like, such as prunes, dried apricots, dried figs, raisins, pears, apples, and peaches, but choose a good mixture and have at least four different varieties.

METRIC/IMPERIAL	AMERICAN
225 g/8 oz dried fruit (see above)	8 oz dried fruit (see above)
2 tablespoons blanched almonds	2 tablespoons blanched almonds
2 tablespoons pine nuts	2 tablespoons pine nuts
1 tablespoon rose water	1 tablespoon rose water
1 tablespoon orange water	1 tablespoon orange water
raw sugar (see below)	raw sugar (see below)

Put the dried fruit into a bowl, just cover with water, then put into a cool place, or into the refrigerator for 48 hours. Stir in the nuts, rose water and orange water and taste the liquor. If it needs it, add a little sugar to taste, but the amount will depend on the sweetness of the fruit. Chill for at least one hour before serving.

Serves 4

Prunes in White Wine

I have always felt that the poor old prune is very much maligned.

'Prunes and custard' said in a dreary tone of voice and 'just like a dried up old prune' hardly conjure up the idea of something delectable to eat, but they are – and with so little effort. A perfect dessert to serve if you are entertaining but will be pressed for time. It can be prepared the day before, and then be forgotten about until you want to serve it.

METRIC/IMPERIAL	AMERICAN
50 g/2 oz sugar	¼ cup sugar
grated rind and juice 1 orange	grated rind and juice 1 orange
300 ml/½ pint white wine	1 ¼ cups white wine
225 g/8 oz prunes	2 cups prunes

Put the sugar, orange rind and juice and wine into a bowl and leave for 10 minutes, stirring occasionally until the sugar has dissolved. Add the prunes, cover with clingwrap and put into the fridge for at least 12 hours or for up to 24.

Serves 4

Prunes with Tea

This recipe is essentially 'prunes de luxe', as there is added alcohol and they are served smothered with whipped cream, but for a more economical version, prunes soaked in tea and served with yogurt is almost as good. You can use any tea you like (China, Indian or herb), but it should not be too strong or it will completely dominate the prunes.

METRIC/IMPERIAL	AMERICAN
225 g/8 oz prunes	2 cups prunes
450 ml/¾ pint tea	2 cups tea
about 20 blanched almonds	about 20 blanched almonds
3 tablespoons dark rum or brandy	3 tablespoons dark rum or brandy
raw sugar (see below)	raw sugar (see below)
150 ml/¼ pint double cream	⅝ cup heavy cream
2 tablespoons single cream	2 tablespoons light cream

Put the prunes into a bowl, pour over the tea and leave to soak for 24 hours. Cut them open with a sharp knife, remove the stones and fill the cavity where the stone was removed with an almond. Add the rum or brandy, to the liquor, then, if it needs a little sugar, add up to about a tablespoon, but it should not be too sweet, as there is plenty of sweetness in the prunes.

Divide the prunes and liquor between four bowls or glasses. Whip the double (heavy) cream and single (light) cream together until it holds its shape. Pile the cream over the prunes and chill for at least one hour before serving.

Serves 4

INDEX